# HOW TO DISCOVER YOUR LIFE'S PURPOSE AFTER 30

---

## WHAT THE FUDGE AM I HERE FOR?

## MIA BOLDEN

# CONTENTS

*This book is dedicated to everyone who believed in me, even when I didn't believe in myself.*

"The two best days
in life are the day you
were born and the day
you discovered why."

Mark Twain

# INTRODUCTION

How to Discover Your Passion & Purpose is a step-by-step guide on doing just that! Let's be real, in school no one really talked about passion or purpose. We were taught (or at least I was) to go to school, make good grades, get into a good college, get a job that pays well, and you'll be successful. And, yes, that does sound good and work for some people, just NOT me!!

If you're like me and many of the women I coach and work with, you'll wake up one day and say, "What the Fudge Am I Here For?!"

Maybe you're at a point in life where you're tired of working the same job day after day, you feel like your talents are not being used, you're ready to make a difference in your career and it not just be another day on the job, or maybe you're going through a major transition in life and you're READY to discover your true Passion & Purpose. If this sounds like you or someone you know this book is for YOU!

I'll see you on the inside! Mia

# 1

## WHO THE FUDGE IS MIA BOLDEN?

What the hell is my "This"?

When I'm saying my "This," I mean your life's purpose...what exactly are you here for? I believe everyone is put on this earth for more than just paying bills. In school we were never really taught our "This." We were taught to go to school, get a job, go to college, make good grades, start a family, pay bills, go home, do it again. At home, my mom and dad were also doing this even though I'm sure they didn't mean to. They'd say, "When you get out and pay your own bills, you'll be grown, but until then you have to do what we say." Of course, as a teenager, I wanted to be grown, so I formed a vision that paying bills equaled adulthood. Nobody talks about what the fudge are we here for!

I call it my "This" or your "This" because life's purpose was too much for me. Saying, "What is your life's purpose" when I started looking for mine, it just seemed too out there. It felt like something that required too much—a higher education that I did not because I dropped out of high school and did not get my GED until the age of 23. I didn't have a clear path of where I was going in life. It just seemed too far out of reach, but finding my "This" was more my style. I mean, when I ask somebody, "What's your This? Do you like to dance? Do you like to go to the club? Do you like to talk? Or, what are you good at? What gets you up in the morning? What are you passionate about?" They could get that. That feels like something they could figure out. "Life's Purpose" feels like something I would never relate to and that's not the language I personally use! Sorry, not sorry, LOL!

In school, people don't ask you what you're good at. It starts there. We are expected to do what everyone else does. We are conditioned to follow a path that may not be right for us, and it can set you up for failure. If you're not good at math, but you are good at cooking and love to cook, it doesn't matter. You still have to do math. This makes you look at other people who are good at math and think, "I'm not as good as her." This may make you just go through life feeling lost and bad about yourself, and this is just one example.

It's not just about finding what you're good at either. When I found my "This", it also led me to helping people, which is more like that Life's Purpose thing people were talking about. But finding my "This" was much more reachable for me.

If I put people who knew me in my past in the same room with people who have only met me after I found my "This", they would say, "What the fudge?" because I truly am a different person. Well, the people who knew me in my twenties might be more like, "What the f*&^?"

When I was eighteen, the lady who had always been my rock

passed away. My grandmother was very special to me and is still a guiding light for me. Her death and other events led me to move to where my grandparents lived in a small town outside of Winston-Salem, North Carolina. I visited my grandpa regularly to make sure he was okay, and I helped with my family. I stepped in and followed what my grandma had taught me, and I became the ringleader of my family.

In North Carolina, I quickly got sucked into the trap of just doing what everybody else does, and I got a job making fast money, which in my case was bartending and waiting tables. I had already been waiting tables back home, so it was easy for me to get a job by transferring to the same restaurant in North Carolina. I really thought that because I was paying my bills and I had my own apartment that I was grown. Remember, that's what my vision of success was back then.

The more money you made, the better you were in my eyes. The messages I got from music, TV, and society in general were telling me that the fast life was equal to success and happiness. All the music videos, reality shows and the people that I was watching and idolizing at the time--that's what they were doing, and that's what I was feeling. So I thought that was the life I wanted.

When an opportunity to sell drugs fell into my lap, I took it. My cousin became the big wig in North Carolina, and he saw an opportunity in me being a female and invited me into his circle. Seeing the piles of money they were making made it easy for me to say yes. They were bringing in loads of dope. It was nothing for me to have pounds of weed in my house at one time. I was the girl you came to if you wanted five pounds, twenty pounds. I became THE dope girl. Who the fudge would have thought?! (As I'm re-reading this before print, I'm laughing at the people who know me now, their jaws are dropping. Pick up your lips people! Yes, I have a past too. Ok, moving on...)

The money flowed in like the liquor I poured. I'm not gonna lie, it was a good life. I got to experience what it was like to have things. I got to eat in nice restaurants. I got to go shopping all the time. I had nice clothes, a nice car, and a nice apartment. I remember one time my lights got cut off. It wasn't because I didn't have the money to pay the bill, I just forgot. Me and my cousin went and rented a room at a five-star hotel to wait until they cut the electricity back on, and I ended up staying there for over a month just because I could.

A typical day in the life of old Mia consisted of what I called "Wake 'n Bake": drink some coffee, check my phone for calls or texts (we didn't have Facebook and all that back then). Then I would jump in my decked out black Dodge Avenger, turn up some music, and go to my day job at the restaurant. I always worked even though I didn't have to. I worked the day shift so that at night I could go make my runs. I would get off and go meet someone at my house or out in the country to drop off or pick up a package. It was a good life. It was a great life. I would go out to eat, shop, and buy more high-end liquor. I did whatever I wanted because I could, and I didn't worry about money.

I had everything I thought I needed, but there was a little tug at me. I felt like I wasn't getting anywhere. Something was missing. I didn't feel fulfilled, but I ignored it.

I've always had leadership in me, but back then I was a leader in doing things I wasn't supposed to do. I had an attitude and a chip on my shoulder. I was quick to cuss someone out in a second if they looked at me wrong or said something stupid. I loved to go out to the country and shoot guns or go to the "Liqua' House" (properly called the "Liquor House" or "Card House"). I would be the only girl at the card table dropping one hundred dollar bills on games. We would play some nights 'til the sun came up. I didn't partake in the hard drugs, but I was around it regularly. It was nothing for people at the card house to be tootin' cocaine all night long.

I felt like I was somebody because people knew who I was. I had money. I had the dope. But when I was alone, I would feel this pull inside of me, a sense of loneliness. It's hard to describe, but you might know that pull that I'm talking about without me using the right words. But sometimes we hush that pull and just move on to our daily lives.

One day I met "The Fool." He was a dope boy. He made a lot of money too. He became a part of my fast life. Being with him made me feel like I was on another level. People knew us. We became a power couple on the streets.

"The Fool" would take me out to fancy restaurants, get my nails and hair done, a bad outfit, the whole nine yards. He'd go make his runs, and I'd be sittin' in his really nice Cadillac thinkin' I'm cute! Then I'd go do my runs. We were regulars at what I call the "Titty Bars" and throw money at the girls like it was nothing. After that, I'd go play my cards with my cousins at the Liqua' House. He'd go off to sleep with some other girl, probably the stripper we'd just been tippin' at the club.

Partying was fun, but I still felt like there was something inside of me that just was not right. I wanted more, but I thought that it was just more money, another trip, another party or another night out, and I would do those things. There was still something missing. I can't even tell you how strong it was and how empty I felt, but I just kept hushing that noise.

We did argue, and I knew he was cheating, but what was important was being that power couple. He never physically abused me or anything, but he was emotionally abusive. He would say stupid stuff, and in fact, I'm sure I slapped him quite a few times. He wouldn't come home, and when he did, I knew he'd been with someone else. He even got his ex-baby's-momma pregnant again during the three years we were together. Like a fool, I stayed with him.

Like an even bigger fool, I said yes when he asked me to marry him. Just one month later, I caught him cheating again, and I was just done. It was three years too long. Two months before he asked me to marry him, my cousin (and supplier) had gotten busted and sentenced to prison for fourteen years. Everything was falling apart around me.

I continued to work hard throughout my twenties without any real goals in mind. I didn't really know where I was going. I didn't have a five-year plan or a ten-year plan. I didn't even think I needed to have a plan for the next year. I just wanted to make sure that I could maintain my lifestyle and just pay my bills. Now, I didn't know how I was going to do that.

Me and "the Fool" went through a bad breakup. It was ugly. And, without my cousin, I did not have access to drugs to sell. Things were changing. My cousins that I'd been there to help were growing up and having their own kids, and I just felt a pull away from that lifestyle of being the ringleader of the family. I knew something was coming, and I just needed to get out of there, out of that environment, out of North Carolina.

Finally, at thirty years old, I had to tuck my tail between my legs and make that dreaded phone call. "Mom? Can I come home?"

I moved back to Pensacola, Florida and started doing what I know--waiting tables and bartending.

All of this led to two major changes--gaining weight and feeling the struggle. I have never been a small girl by any means, but when I got on the scale and it said that I weighed 297 pounds, I was like "Oh My-Lanta!" On top of that, yes I was making decent money, but not the dope girl money I had gotten used to. I had to readjust myself. All the money I had made from the ages 23 to 29 was gone.

I went to work out with my sisters to try to lose some of the weight. Working out was their thing. They liked going to the gym. I can definitely tell you that was not my thing. I did not like the way I looked, and I did not feel comfortable. I felt out of control.

I wanted something fun to do. Then I remembered that they had pole fitness classes in North Carolina, so I checked into that. There weren't any pole fitness classes in Pensacola.

My hustler and entrepreneurial spirit kicked in. I called my friend Rashida, who was a certified Zumba instructor and told her that I wanted to put together a fun hip-hop fitness class. We got together in my living room and created an hour-long workout routine. Then, I rented a building across from where I was working. I knew the owner, and he let me rent it out for one hour one day per week. I went to work on the business side of things--promoting the class, making a website, networking, etc. Ladies started coming to the class, and I knew I was on to something. I liked the way I was feeling--leading, motivating, and inspiring others.

In the meantime, I had fallen in love with yoga, so I decided to get certified and blend this with the classes we were offering. This was when I started really transforming and finding myself. I got my yoga certification in flexibility and slow flow, and I started a class called Sexy Flex. The classes started growing, so we moved into a local community center.

Six months later, I went out on a limb and started my first studio. It felt right. For the first time ever, I felt like I was finally going in the direction of the pull I'd been feeling years ago. It just felt like the right direction.

The ladies in the classes started asking me for pole fitness classes. We started adding burlesque cardio, Buti Yoga and Booty Camp. I met Tina who was a vertical pole fitness instructor from Colorado. She joined my studio and created our vertical pole fitness certification program. We added Vertical Pole Fitness classes to our growing schedule.

Students started opening up to me after class with their personal struggles. Some of them would say things like, "I've been in a marriage for so long, I just don't feel sexy anymore," or "I just don't feel good." I started giving them advice and encouraging them. They would come back and talk about how my advice helped them. I really liked how that made me feel. Something was happening to me on the inside. I was being the leader, the entrepreneur, the hustler I'd always been, but I was becoming something more. Whether it was a class or something I said, I was influencing these women in a positive way. I started feeling better inside. I knew then I was on to something.

I'm a big kid at heart, and I saw all these women being empowered, getting stronger, and having fun. So I decided to get certified and I fell in love with teaching pole fitness. I started incorporating pole fitness with advice which led to coaching before I even knew what coaching was.

I didn't know at the time that the emptiness, that pull I was feeling was going to lead me to becoming a Vertical Pole Studio Owner and Instructor, Motivational Speaker, and Empowerment Coach. If you would have told me that this would be my life when I was twenty-five, I would have looked at you and laughed in your face! I wish that I had not hushed that noise that was trying to tell me I was in the wrong place. I wish that I had not wasted so much time and money. I wish I would have listened to that pull inside years ago.

If I could go back, I would definitely have made other choices and invested some of that money. We can't go back, but we can move forward and be grateful for those past experiences. My past has made me an easy person to open up to. I'm not judgmental, and I can understand struggles because I've been there and done that. This all brought me to where I am today. I know that I've found my "This". I've never felt as right as I do right now.

I was pulled to my "This", and now I truly believe everyone else is being pulled too. If you are feeling like something is missing, that's because it is. Instead of having everything fall apart around you to make you listen, I hope that you will start searching for your "This" right now.

## 2

## HOW I FOUND MY "THIS"

I was at a pretty low point in my life. I had gained weight, weighing in around 300 pounds - the heaviest I had ever been. I had just moved back home to Florida, waiting tables and bartending again. I just wasn't feeling good about myself. I believe that things are just drawn to you at the right time. One night, I was at home scrolling through YouTube videos, and a motivational video popped up. It was Les Brown, who I had never heard of before. He has become my number one motivational speaker and mentor.

My man Les was just talking about Life's Purpose, which I had heard about but never gave two seconds to think about. He was talking about how we all have this purpose in life and how as kids we naturally know what we want to do in life. I was like, "What? As kids we know?" This caught my attention. As kids, he said, we have this imagination, but at certain times (in school or in other areas of life) people have you hush that.

For instance, I've always been a talker. In school, I was always told to be quiet. I was always getting in trouble for talking. Just imagine if at that time, someone had helped me develop my speaking skills. I can't imagine where I'd be right now if someone would have helped me work on public speaking, grammar, and leading through speaking when I was younger. I'd be a bad mother-shut-your-mouth speaker in the speaking world today. Our natural talents are suppressed because we have to work on our basic studies and learn how to "act properly."

But, by whose standards? I know we have to know the basics and we have to understand the rules of society, but a lot of our natural talents have nothing to do with that. Take someone who likes to listen to music all day. When they were little, that's what they liked to do-listen to music all the time. But in school, teachers and parents do not see listening to music as something you should focus on.

So they get the child to focus on school work. "Make good grades," they say, "so you can graduate and go on to a good college." And if you're one of the lucky ones, you follow what the teacher and parents say. And we get into that college, we follow a career path that society says is acceptable, and makes good money to pay those bills. Then twenty years later, they're in a career that they're not happy in and are screaming, "I don't want to do this! What the fudge am I here for?!"

That video of Les Brown that I came across really started to work on me. It made me think about what I naturally love to do, and that's when I put pen to paper and started writing. I made a list of what I naturally like to do. I like to talk. I like to lead. I like to travel. I like to dance. I like to make people laugh. I realized that these were things that I enjoyed doing as a kid but that they had been hushed. When I realized this, I started feeling better. That video was like the day that you go to church even though you don't really want to, but the preacher starts preaching, and you feel like he's talking directly to you. He's saying exactly what you needed to hear!

Then, meditating happened. I say it happened because I never expected it. In the beginning when people started telling me about meditating and how it would help me, I was probably like, 98% of the people I was hanging around at the time, and I thought it was crazy. I was like, "Black people don't meditate!" Truly, I never thought it was something that would benefit me or that it would be something good for me to do.

Like I said, I started exercising. I went to my first yoga class – not just any yoga class, but a hot yoga class. What the fudge was I thinking?! I had heard a lot about yoga and how you can free your mind, and I thought I'd give it a try.

I almost died. I was like, "What the fudge is this? People do this for enjoyment?" At the end of the class, when we were in Shavasana pose, I just started crying. I didn't know why I was crying, but I remember feeling that something was going on inside of me, and it was good. I felt like I was releasing the parts of myself that I needed to let go of, not just physically but mentally.

I also started watching other motivational videos and speakers, and one of the things that they had in common was meditating. For me at first, I was following my new vision success. They all talked about journaling and meditation. Success leaves clues, you better pay attention!

These two things prompted me to start meditating. I did believe in the power of the mind. My grandmother always talked about how powerful your mind is. I had just never tried to practice anything to tap into that power. And, I thought, if these successful people are all doing it, there must be something to it. At this point in my life, I was really tired of trying to figure out things on my own. I was ready to listen, be a student, and take action with the steps other successful people were taking.

I started simple with meditating. I would wake up early and set my phone timer for four minutes, and I would just lay there or sit on my bed. It took me a couple of months to be able to just sit there, be quiet, and quiet my mind. At first, I had all that noise going on in my head - "Oh, God, I have a meeting," or "I've got to do this," "I've got to do that." Eventually, I was able to get quiet and calm down, and this truly changed me.

I realized that I needed to start working on myself beyond just losing weight and figuring out what I wanted to do with my life. I needed to figure out who I really wanted to be. I needed to quiet my mind and start working on myself from the inside out.

I started actually looking things up on Youtube about success, and another thing that kept popping up was journaling. All of these successful people would talk about how they write things down and journal. As I started meditating and journaling, I saw things more clearly of the direction that I wanted to go towards in my life.

Guess what happened? My "This" came to me. I started seeing how I really liked helping women, and this opened up the avenue of empowering women and changing their lives beyond fitness coaching and exercise.

Now, when I first started listening to Les Brown, I didn't really want to be a speaker. I was just like, "Oh my man here is motivating me," and I liked the way it made me feel.

But, the more I meditated and journaled, the more I realized that these things were coming to me for a reason – motivating, speaking, helping women, making people laugh, and coaching. So I was like, "What the fudge? Let me try that out!"

I went from being at that low point in my life and feeling like I didn't know what to do, to having direction. I went from being angry and having an attitude to learning how to let stuff roll off my back. If I can come from being the dope girl and staying at the liqua house all night to meditating, journaling, and finding my "This", anyone can!

All of this led me to the path of being an Empowerment Coach. I was coaching women in the fitness classes and inspiring them, so I became a Certified Life Coach. I was empowering women to feel good about their bodies. Then I realized that my clients needed even more than that. They needed to find their "This" and be held accountable to reaching their goals. This is what led me to becoming an Empowerment Coach. Now I help empower women, guide them toward their" This", help them step into their greatness, and rock their lives like the boss babes that they are!

## 3

---

# CALM DOWN & THINK!

Taking time to meditate, journal, and get quiet.

Together we have work to do! Pen and paper, my friends, is what I want you to grab here. And if you don't have any paper, I got you! Turn to the end of this chapter – I've left a couple of blank pages just for you!

Let's start putting this into action. You know I'm a lady who likes to make lists. I always tell people, "If it ain't written, it ain't real." This process is going to be a little bit of both meditating and journaling. I really want you to take the time. Go into a room and be still. One of my favorite quotes is, "Silence has so much to say." See what comes up and just start writing. It doesn't even need to make sense. Trust the process.

Now let's talk meditation. Don't think you have to do it for 20-30 minutes. I started off meditating 3-4 minutes. I would set the alarm on my phone, and just be in a quiet space and things started coming to me. I want you to try that. Start off by meditating for a few minutes a day and see what happens.

Your natural talents have been hushed. You were told, "Hush, and go back to your math problem." "Hush and get back to work." You may have been daydreaming about your "This" and what you're naturally good at, but someone hushed you. With meditation, you get to reclaim your "This". You get to quiet down all the other noise and listen to your inner voice.

It probably won't be easy at first. You'll need to unclutter that big to-do list that you have on a daily basis (going to work, going to practice, etc.). It may be hard to take a minute to really just sit and think. Just allow your mind to start daydreaming again like when you were a child. Sit and allow things to come to you that will help you find your purpose and keep you on track.

You may think that you don't have time to meditate or you can't meditate with your partner or your family around. It's different strokes for different folks. You just have to make the time and space for it! Now let's get it!

First of all, don't go into the mediation thinking that you're going to feel some type of way when you get done or having expectations. Second, find what works for you. Some people do it before they even get out of bed, my favorite way. They lay quietly pretending to be asleep. You can even get on the toilet and close your eyes. You might do it in the car right before you go into the office. If you have trouble blocking everything out, you can try guided meditation. There are apps, or you can find YouTube videos – that's what I did. Eventually, the more you do it, the noise will go away. Just focus on sitting and being still. It took me a couple of months to be able to clear my mind without thinking, "Oh my god, I've got a meeting."

Another thing is to trust the process. I'm going to repeat that:

Trust the process. As silly as it sounds, it works. You may think this is crazy, but I'm telling you, just trust the process. Trust me, ideas will start coming to you and push you in the right direction. Meditating can be used for many things, but for the purpose of finding your "This", it's just about clearing your head so you can start letting new ideas flow into your mind.

The closest thing to meditating that I ever knew was my uncle practicing Buddhism. He would sit in front of his Buddha and meditate, but that was just one time in my life that I had seen someone close to me meditate. I understand how it may be new or awkward for some people, or some of you may even be wanting to jump into a full-on meditating practice.

Grab that pen and start writing whatever comes to mind when you think about your "This". Think of people who inspire you, things you might want to do, what you naturally like to do, what you're naturally good at, what you can imagine that you'd like to do for the rest of your life--stuff like that. Start writing it down and see what happens.

Start thinking about the future: What do you want to be doing five to ten years down the road? It's not necessarily what you're going to be doing as far as your job or your life's purpose but think more about what kind of feelings you want to have. Do you want to be motivated? Do you want to be fulfilled? Do you want to have fun? Do you want to travel? Do you want a family?

Also think about the environment that you want to be in. What kind of house do you want to have? Do you want to have that big mansion? Do you want more of a small, southern type home, like a log cabin? What kind of life do you want to live?

Think about what kind of relationships you want to be in, what kind of health. Don't necessarily go in there thinking that you're going to find your life's purpose, but just focus on what you want and how you want to feel.

Put those things in your list. Now, this list may take a while. This may not happen in one or two sessions. It might take you a week; it may take you a month or even three months. Because this is something that we normally don't think about, it may take time and practice to figure it out.

As of right now, I don't know what I'm going through, but I've been watching Van Lifers and I love how they have the freedom to hop in their van and travel from state to state. All of that came up for me when I was meditating and journaling. That's the kind of stuff I want you to focus on, what makes you feel good, and the how you get there will come later.

Just sit there and make lists and write down whatever comes to mind. Turn everything off, sit and see what happens. You'll be amazed at the ideas that come to you.

You'll start seeing connections between the way you feel and what you like and things that you can do. Maybe you like dogs, and you think, "I could be a dog-walker." Write that down. There are people making bank right now being professional dog walkers. Maybe you used to like to paint, but life has gotten in the way. Write that down. Maybe painting is your natural talent. Maybe you think, "I like to dress people; I'm good at putting together outfits." Some people are not good at that and pay people to help them find fashionable outfits. You may even say, "I like to shop." People get paid ridiculous amounts of money to shop for others. Whatever it is, write it down. It's all part of the process. At this point, it's all about discovery: getting back to who you are and what you really like to do.

Writing things down starts putting things into motion. It's not something that you will see...Maybe you write down, "I want to make a million dollars." You will put things into motion just by writing it down. You may not see it immediately, but I promise, this will make a difference.

Believe me, I'm not a big writer. I'm definitely more of a talker. It took time for me to get into writing stuff down, but when I started journaling, I remember I wrote down, "travel, make a lot of money, taste a lot of different foods, dance, teach, learn, help women." I even wrote down that I wanted to have a specific amount of money. The real deal is that all of these things have either happened or are happening now. I've seen it all come to life. I'm traveling more in the past two years than I have in the past ten years. I just came back from Bali hosting my first International women's empowerment retreat. I'm trying different restaurants. I'm speaking all over the US at different conference, retreats and workshops. What's crazy is that I've done things I did not even realize I wanted to do that were connected to this list. For instance, the show "Diners, Drive-ins, and Dives" is my show, and I always said that I want to eat at one of those restaurants. Did I mention I was a big foodie? I was recently speaking in South Carolina, Chicago and Georgia. In each of those cities, I ended up eating a restaurant that was on the show!

All these things that I wrote down are happening. You have to trust the process. You may not know why you're writing down what you're writing down, but it is all part of the process. Eventually, it will all come together. But, you have to start somewhere, and clearing your head and getting down to business is a good place to start. It will help you block out the noise so you can gain clarity on the direction of your life and help you discover your "This". Now let's get to work!

**Brain Dump: What Comes to Me in My Quiet Time?**

## 4

## LET'S TALK NATURAL TALENT!

You Betta Work! (In My Rupaul Voice)

Finding your natural talent is something that we don't think about, especially as an adult because our lives have been programmed differently. We stop thinking about things we like to do because we have to think about "reality." I want you take a minute, dig down deep, breathe, and just think about when you were a child. What did you naturally like to do? Sing, play, build things, play in the dirt, do your sister's hair – what was your thing? What was the thing that put a smile on your face, and sometimes you would get in trouble for doing it but you turned around and did it anyways?

I'm gonna use myself as an example. Like I said, I've always been a talker. When I was younger, I REALLY liked to talk. I talked all the time...I was actually the class clown. I remember getting in trouble -- "Jamilha stop talking, Jamilha be quiet, Jamilha you're talking too loud." That pretty much happened to me from elementary school until I dropped out of high school. That made me feel bad, it made me feel like I was a bad student. I was like, "Man, I'm always getting in trouble," but I was just being myself.

My teachers always made phone calls to my mom or sent notes home. I even got put out of the class for talking. Getting in trouble all the time for talking made me feel like I was a bad student, but I enjoyed talking and was good at it. Being told that I needed to stop talking did not help me, nor did it make me stop. It just made me feel bad about myself, and it hushed my natural talent of my gift of gab which I can confidently now say is a gift. Do you know how many people are afraid of public speaking, getting out there and meeting new people, or making the sale because they are afraid to speak up? Not me! I'm just sayin'...

I also wanted to lead. I'll never forget as a child I wanted the lead role in whatever we were playing. If we were playing store, then I wanted to be the cashier because I thought she was in charge. If we were playing school, I wanted to be the teacher who was leading the students. These are things that I was naturally good at, but as I went through school and life, it got hushed.

Instead of saying, "Hey, this girl likes to talk, let's let her do the announcements," or teach her some public speaking skills, they just told me to be quiet. I probably would have been good at taking charge, and this could have helped me find my "This" earlier, but it got hushed.

I remember this boy who got in trouble for playing with paperclips. All the time, he was always building things with whatever he could find. Remember McGuyver? That was him! He may have been using his imagination to design something. They could have honed in on his talents and help him invent something.

I also remember a girl in middle school who was always doing someone's hair. She wasn't thinking about science. She was thinking about doing hair, and she was good at it. I don't know where she ended up, but it would be a shame if she was pushed in another direction that was not her true talent.

Yes, you have to learn how to control yourself in certain settings, but your talents should not be hushed. You should explore the things that come naturally to you and see where they will lead you.

There are a lot of people who experienced this as well. For instance, a friend of mine was always daydreaming. She was always exploring and thinking about going to other places, but she also got in trouble for that. Her parents used to say, "You can go once you get a job and can afford that." She is now a nurse and barely ever travels. She could have been an archeologist. She may have become a travel journalist. Instead, she was pushed away from her natural talent.

What if your natural talents were hushed? Let's find out.

Now I want you to find your natural talent. Think about what you naturally liked to do when you were growing up. It may seem silly. You may have liked to sing in the shower. You may have liked to play a leading role in the school play. You may have been like me and loved talking.

Write it down. There is no right or wrong answer here.

It's also good to even think about asking a long-time friend or family member that is really cool with you and will keep it real with you.

"What do you think that I'm good at?" If you're brave, you'll ask them what they think your weaknesses are – write those down as well. And remember, love them anyways when they hit you with the real deal.

Maybe they say, "You were really good at gymnastics. "You know when we used to do those flips in the backyard." Maybe that will help you out if you're getting stuck.

When you think about what you're naturally good at, also think about what you naturally do good for other people. I can sit here and motivate you for nine hours straight, and lose track of time. I don't ever want to stop motivating and helping people. I live for it.

I know I keep going back to me a lot, but I am the one writing the book, LOL!

Another way to think about it is *Is it 5 o'clock already?!" -- What can you do and get lost in time?

You're going to start seeing a common denominator, and something is going to fit. Sometimes it may not be this big "Ah Hah," like Mia's going to be a speaker and a coach. It's more about just putting stuff out there and trusting the process. My definition of success is to do something that you love and get paid to do it." When you find something that you can get lost in, something that feels good, and something that comes naturally, that's your "This".

Last but not least, write down what you can do all day and not get paid for it. It doesn't need to make sense now, but it will – trust the process. My list went something like this: travel, motivating people, eat food, exploring the wilderness, and making people laugh. Now turn the page, and get to writing!

**What Is My Natural Talent?**

# 5

## WE ALL NEED SOMEONE TO LOOK UP TO!

Let's talk about people who have inspired and motivated you in your life.

Let's go back into that quiet room and make another list. Think about who is that person(s) who has/have inspired you. Having a mentor or two to look up to is great for motivation, inspiration, and endurance. You don't have to copy that person, but you should have someone to guide you even if they don't know they're doing it.

I have been blessed to have a few strong people in my life who have inspired me and who I can really say that have qualities that I have picked out to replicate.

My grandmother Christine is an example. She was a boss babe. I liked to watch her leadership skills. She was into politics. My grandmother was a little five-foot Hawaiian Chinese lady in this room with big, strong men in suits. She would go up there and either debate or pump up the crowd. I would be like "Dang! Check her out!" I knew then that I wanted to command attention like she did. Here she was this small little woman...She had on her Hawaiian Moo-Moo dress, and she was comfortable. Even though she may not have looked the part, when she spoke, people listened. She was a leader by just being herself, dressing the way she did, and talking the way she did with her broken English Hawaiian accent. Even though she didn't look like everyone else in the room, you could hear a pin drop when she spoke – everyone listened.

When I remembered this, I recognized that I have that voice that can carry, and I know that I got that from her. That has inspired me in my speaking today.

Here's the point: When I was thinking about my This, I always thought you had to take a lot of actions, but really what you need to do is work from the inside out! Every time I think about this, I think about my grandmother saying, "It's all in your mind, discipline your mind." This came up when I started making my lists. It really started making sense. Before, I didn't know what she meant when she said discipline your mind. But when you are starting to work on yourself, you really have to work hard to discipline yourself mentally first. My grandmother not only inspired my speaking, but she also inspired my leadership skills. She always told me to be a leader, not a follower, and to speak up for yourself and others. I used to be the one in school who would bully the bullies, and speak up for those who couldn't speak up for themselves.

Think about the people that inspire you - write them down. Then, write down what you admire about them. Write down how they inspired you, what skills and talents they had that you liked, so you can look at it and follow their example, be encouraged, and find inspiration.

My grandfather James owned his own business. I liked the fact that he didn't go to a traditional job. I loved that he made his own hours and was his own boss. At the time, I didn't even know then that I wanted to own my own business. I just knew that I respected my grandfather. Now, I look at how he ran his business. I just saw the freedom he had and how family and friends looked up to him for being a business owner. I used to admire how people wanted to be around him. He had that unspoken energy – I wanted that. I respected my grandfather for those things and so much more.

If you start looking at the people who inspire you, this will help you. You're looking at them to see what it is about them that you admire. Don't think that you're looking at them to be like them but you're trying to find the things that do inspire you and motivate you to become a better version of yourself.

Now turn the page and write down at least five people you've looked up that have inspired you and in what way.

**Five People I Look Up to and Why**

# 6

## TRUST YO' SELF!

Listen to your thoughts & intuition.

A lot of us go to work five to six days a week just because we are in the mindset of just paying bills. We may be miserable at work and hate what we do, but we don't listen to that voice inside of us that's telling us, "Hey, there's something more out there for you!"

We are the only species that will not listen to our intuition. When animals have an instinct, they follow it naturally. When humans have an instinct inside of them to go to that job interview, make the call, ask for the help – instead of doing that, we don't listen to that voice on the inside and tend to do the opposite.

I always worried about paying bills and making money, and those were my main goals pretty much all my life. I've done everything from waiting tables, hustling, bartending, retail, cleaning hotels, you name it, I've done it. But I always knew that there was something inside of me telling me that there's more out for you sista!

For the first time, I was starting to feel fulfilled. When I was at the studio helping women and empowering them, I finally started listening to that pull. When I stopped working home healthcare and bartending, I went through all the trials and tribulations of being a new business owner. For example, not having enough money to pay my bills, working long hours, lack of support, and having no social life. I was scared to take that leap of faith. I was extremely nervous but everything on the inside told me I was doing the right thing. I knew that this was right.

I had never had that feeling before with bartending or home healthcare or anything else that I did. I had never had that drive telling me that I was on the right path. My empty pockets may have told me I was broke as heck, but something inside of me was changing. I knew that this was right for me. We all have that inner intuition and guide, a higher power, but we are scared to take that leap of faith. We're scared to take action because we're focused on the struggles that are right in front of us. Once we do, though, nothing can stop us, and we just know it is right.

All of the great leaders, business owners, and successful people, all the people that have found their "This", they did it. They followed their gut. They did not listen to what everybody else said, what society said, or what their parents told them. They blocked out what others said that they should be doing or could be doing, and they followed their intuition.

Even growing up, I always knew that I was supposed to be a leader. I always knew that I was destined to be in charge or work for myself. I always felt that. I've always felt that I was a leader and a teacher in some sense. I just didn't know who I was supposed to be leading or teaching, so I just went along with society just like everybody else.

It is a statistical fact that most heart attacks happen on Mondays between the hours of eight and twelve. I believe that this is directly related to the fact that people are going to work on Monday mornings at a job where they don't feel fulfilled. They're at a job that they don't like. They're working 10-, 12-, 14-hours at this job, and there's something telling them to stop.

We all have that point in life. Something tells us, "Maybe you should look into going back to school," or "Maybe you should look into going into the military." But we just continue to worry about Monday morning, getting to that dead-end job that we don't like or doesn't utilize our skills, talents, or knowledge, and we are physically making ourselves sick. When we don't listen to our intuition, to our gut, our bodies start manifesting physical symptoms.

When I finally started listening to my gut, I found my path. That path even led me to another path. It was like a domino effect, and it all started when I stopped listening to what everyone else said or watching what everyone else did and started doing what was right for me.

On the next page, I want you to write down a few things you've wanted to try but you talked yourself out of doing it before you even began. Don't worry, no one else is going to see this list but you!

Remember, we are working from the inside out!

# Things I Want to Do but Haven't Tried Yet

# 7

## LEARN TO LAUGH AT FEAR!

What would you do if you were fearless?

You have more control over your thoughts and feelings than you think you do. So when you start feeling fear, just change it and say, "I am so excited!" Use that feeling and say, "I'm going to rock this out like a Boss," or say, "I Got This!" This will change that energy from negative into positive.

How many of you are going to work and just going through the motions? How many of you clock-in and clock-out just because that's what you do every day? You know that you have talents that you are not using. You go to work five to six days a week, forty plus hours, feeling that pull inside of you, but you just go to your job because that's what you did yesterday.

We only have one life. We only have one shot at this. What are you going to do with yours? Are you going to sit in the corner cowering? Or are you going to face that fear and just do it? Try to find your "This", follow your intuition, and see where it takes you? You want to live full and die empty.

Think about what gets you out of bed in the morning. If it's because you have to go to work and get the kids ready for school, then that might be a reason for you to get back in bed LOL! Your "This" will drive you to get up. You'll want to get up and get ready to start your day because every day excites you! You go to work because you're doing what you love and you can't wait to get there!

When I wanted to start speaking, I had already opened the studio and I was coaching the women without even really knowing I was doing life coaching. I've always been a talker (as we all know!), and I've always known that I was a leader. If you've never made a vision board, you absolutely should! When I made my first one, I put on my vision board a picture of me standing at a podium acting like I was speaking to a room full of people. I wrote on the picture, "I am a funny, highly energetic, inspirational motivational speaker and leader. I Got This."

Two weeks later, a colleague of mine asked me to speak at the local battered women's shelter. I was excited, and I wanted to do it. But, when I got home, I was really freaking out because I had never given a speech before. The group of women really needed someone to really inspire them. I almost didn't do it because I was so scared. I just went and did it anyway.

There was a lady in front of me, and she just started crying. I didn't know if that was a good thing or what, but after I was finished, she came up and thanked me and told me how much I had inspired her. This was the beginning of my speaking career. Speaking engagements started opening up. People started coming to me because they heard how I spoke, asking me to speak at their events. Once you start putting your faith into it and start taking action, things will fall into place.

"Our life is our gift from God. What we do with our life is our gift to God." Once you start following your path, things will open up for you and you'll be rewarded.

If my 20-year-old self and my 30-year-old self met each other, it would be crazy. You never know where your life is going to take you. You just have to face your fears, listen to your gut, and do it anyway!

Fear was holding me back from just jumping into my business. I get it. I was fearful that people would talk about me and say, "Mia's crazy. She doesn't know anything about fitness. She's overweight herself. How can she be a fitness instructor?" All of those things were playing over and over in my head until I actually went out there and did it. You just have to put yourself out there and just do it. You have to feel the fear and do it anyway. I believe that's how you have to overcome the fear. Like Nike says, "Just Do It!" So, if it's a question of "am I going to be able to make it?" no matter what you want to do from being a writer, a teacher, a dancer, a hairstylist, whatever, if you keep asking yourself, "Am I going to be able to make it?" - you'll never know until you just get out there and do it. The more you take action on your goals, the more that fear will start chiseling away.

Don't think that you have to quit your job at first to pursue something else and follow your passion, but you do need to try new things. If you are worried about finances, or you have responsibilities and you can't take the risk, try different things. Maybe try to volunteer at a dance school as a dance teacher's assistant if opening up a dance studio is your dream. Maybe try volunteering at a hospital if you want to get into medicine. Maybe volunteer at an attorney's office if you're interested in law. Doing this will help you get rid of that fear and boost your confidence. You'll start believing in yourself more because you're really utilizing your talents and letting your passion come out. That's something that will naturally happen once you get on the right path.

You'll know when the time is right. You'll just feel it. It goes back to trusting your intuition. You keep evaluating the way you feel. If you say, "I love the way this feels. I love the way it feels when I'm doing this," then you'll know that you're on the right path. It's like with me and the fitness studio, it felt like that. I loved the way it felt when I was empowering those women, and that calling just kept getting louder and louder. Once that happens, you'll just be ready to take that extra leap of faith and just do it!

Another way to get over that fear is to surround yourself with mentors. Find people who are doing what you want to do or who are just successful and ask them questions. Find out how they got started in their business. Listen to their processes and see what happened with them. Doing that helped me when I started my own business. It helped me to hear that they failed and hear that they struggled. It helped me, as sad as this sounds, to know that I wasn't the only one whose lights got cut off at home because I was worried about bills at the office. Talking to people who had gone through some of the same struggles and made it to the other side really helped me overcome my fear and just say, "Okay. This is a part of the process."

After I took that leap of faith, let me say that everything was not S-H-I-T-S and giggles. In fact, I still have my days when I struggle. In the beginning it was really hard. My lights literally did get cut off. I really had no electricity. I had to focus more on listening to my intuition and not what was in my pocket (or what wasn't in my pocket for that matter). I went from making $200-$300 from a double or even just one good night shift as a bartender to much less, and my wallet was telling me there was something wrong while my gut was saying I was absolutely on the right path.

When I really went full-time at the studio, I didn't pay myself for the first three years of being in business. I was blessed to live in my family home, and although my mama was always hounding me about rent money, I still knew I'd have a roof over my head and friends and family to feed me. As far as food, I remember going to the restaurant where I used to work after working at the studio all day. I would paint and work all day because I did everything myself. I didn't have money to hire contractors, so I was in there learning how to paint and lay flooring along with my cousin and some close friends. I call the owner of that restaurant my aunt because she is like family. I'd go up there because I didn't have money for food, and she'd feed me. There were times when my gas got cut off, and I didn't have any heat in my house. These are things that people don't see about the process, but they happen.

As these things were going on, as bad as it sounds, it still felt right. Like I said, I had my days, and I wasn't always running around being fake with a big smile on my face, and half the time I was like, "What the fudge am I doing?" But, nine times out of ten, I felt better about myself and what I was doing. I felt like my talents were getting used. I was on my journey to my life's purpose without even really knowing my "This" but just knowing that it felt right.

A big part of knowing that what I was doing was right even

when I wasn't making a dime, was the rewards that came from doing what I was doing. When the women would come back and they would cry because they would say that their confidence had been boosted, or they feel beautiful again, or their marriage is better because of what my classes had done for them, - that was all the payment I needed.

When you find your "This" and you're on the right path, it's no longer just about you, but it's also about how you can give back to others. You might be struggling because you're going to school to be a doctor and all your bills are piling up, but when you get there, you'll know you're on the right path because of how you help others. If you're a hairstylist, and you finally make that leap of opening up your own salon, when your customers tell you how you make them feel beautiful, that will show you that you've found your "This". Whatever it is, your "This" is not just about you and how you feel, but it's how you make others feel and how you help others. Some people may just think, "Me, Me, Me," and, yes, I do want you to write a lot about how you feel and what you want to do, but we also have to think about how we can give back to others.

There will always be moments of doubt. I still have those moments to this day. It may not be doubt about being on the right path, but it may be doubt about timing, like questioning why you didn't do it sooner. It may be doubt about other things too, like about smaller decisions. However, once you find your "This", you'll be able to overcome that doubt because your intuition will tell you you're on the right path. You'll be able to recognize the difference between doubt that means something (like you're doing the wrong job) and doubt that is just nervousness that comes from taking a leap of faith.

Once you find your "This", your higher power will reward you. Not to get spiritual or anything, but the Bible says, "For I know the plans I have for you,' declares the Lord, 'plans to prosper you and not to harm you, plans to give you hope and a future" (Jeremiah 29:11). Although it may be difficult, just know that you will not find your "This" and never prosper from it. Stay on your path, and know that the reward will come.

> Let us not become weary in doing good, for at the proper time we will reap a harvest if we do not give up.
>
> — GALATIANS 6:9

*People who have truly found their greatness (their "This") have failed many times. They tried and tried again. They even tried something else until they found what works.

Without the studio, I would have never found my passion for coaching and speaking. I definitely want to hold onto the studio as long as I can because I know what it does for the women and I love teaching. That is where my passion was born, but it has evolved into much more like speaking, coaching, webinars, and more. I would not have found all of that if I had not taken that leap. So, trying different things may lead you to something else.

You will fail your way to success, you will fail your way to your greatness, you will fail your way to your "This".

Growth happens outside of your comfort zone.

Do things that excite you and give you butterflies and make you feel like, "I just did that!" And, when fear creeps up on you, just laugh your way through it feel the fear, and do it anyway!

On the next page, I want you to write down: What are you afraid of when it comes to following your dreams? And answer the question!

**What Am I Afraid of When It Comes to Following My Dreams?**

# 8

## LIFE'S MISSION STATEMENT

What are you here for?

What the fudge is a life's mission statement?" is what was going through my head the first time I heard it when my coach and mentor asked me if I had one. I've heard of a mission statement for a company but never for my life!

As far as your life's mission statement and what you're here for, I had never heard of a life's mission statement until I started working on my own life improvement journey & trying to figure out my "This". My coach told me the purpose of having a life's mission statement is the same as the purpose of a company having one. It helps you see where your focus is. This made total sense.

For example, when I worked at Tuesday's, I remember that the mission statement there was to provide a convenient, upscale, quality experience at an affordable price point. I eventually became a corporate trainer at Tuesday's, and I learned that the mission statement had a huge purpose. This is to let everyone know and remember the values that the company is built on. It provides a foundation and a means of reflection.

I started researching some other things like Nike's mission statement, which is to inspire and innovate every athlete in the world. I started researching people that I admire like my girl Oprah Winfrey. Her mission statement is to be a teacher and to be known for inspiring her students more than they thought that they could be. That one definitely hit me because I'm all about empowering women and just showing them their worth. I help women step into their greatness to rock their life like a Boss and to let them know that they can follow their dreams and build whatever life they want. I knew that was going to be a part of my mission statement. When I read that about Oprah, it just really absolutely clicked with me.

I also looked up Mary Kay's mission statement, which is all about one woman's dream to enrich women's lives. To help women succeed, help change the lives of women and children in need and provide jobs to women around the world.

A strong mission statement allows a company, a brand, a person to establish their values and make sure that everything - the products they sell, the services they provide, and the work that they do aligns with their mission statement. If they are faced with something that does not follow their mission statement, they simply do not do it.

Everything starts in our minds. You have to have a foundation, you have to get it in your mind. You have to know that's what you're here for. This is how I see it, we should discover our passion and our purpose first. Then you will have a vision of how you would like your life to be from that vision. Then you'll be able to set your goals. I believe we set goals based off of our current situation. I believe we need to find our "This" first.

Your mission statement helps you get on track and when things are thrown at you, you'll have a foundation. As we go through life, things change, and yes, your mission statement might change as well, but you'll have a foundation. I know a lot of women who are on boards and serving on committees, or they want to try to help their friend do this or that, and they just really spread themselves too thin. I tell them that they really need to have a foundation. Having a mission statement will help you say "No" a lot easier if you have a foundation in your mind and say, "Is this aligning with my life's mission statement? Is this going to get me closer to my goals, closer to where I want to go, or is it pulling me away from there?" When I was told this, it absolutely made sense.

Not only that, but there are going to be times in your life when your friends or your family will try to influence you. For instance, your family may have a medical background. You may have nurses or doctors or some other type of medical professionals in your family, and you may feel pressured to follow in those footsteps because it feels like you should just naturally do that and that's what everybody else in the family does. If that's not in your heart, or if you're not passionate about it, it will not be what you are really meant to do.

If you sit down and create your life's mission statement, you won't let that influence you. You won't let their influence persuade you. You also won't let their decisions make you feel bad. They chose their path, and you must choose yours. Your mission statement will help you see that more clearly and give you that foundation, that "why".

It's the same thing with your friends. God bless them! I love them to death, but some of their mission statements are not aligned with the mission statement that I have going on right now, but that does not bother me. Whether it's a social event or hanging out with certain groups of friends, or doing certain things, if it's not aligned with getting me closer to my mission, my goals that I've set for myself, I just won't do it as I have no problem saying "No." Some of my friends, like those women I mentioned earlier, do not have this foundation, and I watch them waste time at meetings and networking events that are not aligned with their mission. Having a mission statement will allow you to sit down and have a reference to make sure you are not wasting your time.

Another reason for creating a life's mission statement is that you may have things, like jobs, that present themselves to you. You may be offered a promotion, but if that promotion is not aligning with your life's mission statement, you should avoid it. Even if it seems like a good opportunity, it may just be another block in the road. For example, let's say you want to travel, but you're in a corporate job making good money. You're working all these crazy hours, and on top of that, they offer you a promotion to make even more money. However, the promotion means that you will have to work more hours. You won't get to spend time with your friends and family, and you definitely won't be traveling. Having your life's mission statement in place will help you see that this offer may sound good, but it does not align with your mission of traveling. You might say, "Thank you for the offer, I appreciate it very much, but I cannot accept it at this time." Your mission statement will help you say "No" more easily, and it will help align you with where you want to go.

I believe a lot of times that the outside world runs our life. That is why most of us do not find our passion and our purpose. I'm gonna go back, and I'm gonna say this word probably fifty times in this chapter: We don't have our foundation set. From the time we get up, get out of bed and we start checking Facebook or social media or turning on the news, whatever the case may be, the outside world is influencing where it is that we're gonna go and what is going to be our next step.

I always say this: we are always programming our mind, whether it's consciously or subconsciously. So, if you don't consciously program your mind, to wherever it is that you want to go in life, you will just be doing what the outside world tells you. Consciously programming your mind is constantly doing these steps to find your passion, finding your purpose and reminding yourself of these. I have talked about meditation and affirmations, and that is the subconscious programming. When you say your mission statement over and over, on a daily basis, this will program it into your mind. If you don't do that, you might go after that job because that's what looks good. It may be what your friends or your family members are telling you to do, or that may be where you see all the recognition going, or it may be that there's a lot of money involved. It may just look good and glamorous, so you go in that direction for these reasons without knowing what you really want.

A lot of my coaching clients have done this. They've made similar decisions because something looks good on paper. They've finished college, got the dream job, have a dream car. Some of them are even married with kids, but they are just not fulfilled because they have done what everybody else said they should do instead of setting their foundation and doing it based on what they want to do.

Once you know why you're here, you have to establish your

goals. It helps to see where you're going. This will help you get on track so that when life throws something at you, you'll know whether it's aligned with your purpose or not.

The mission statement also helps you when you're making decisions in your life. Whether it's the next move you want to make, the partner you want to marry, if you want to have kids, if you want to go into business, if you want to go to school, if you want to change your major, or whatever the fudge the case may be, when you know your mission statement, it really helps you align those decisions with where you're trying to go in life.

I just really realized that I had to sit down and write out what my mission statement is in my life. I knew the direction that I wanted to take, and I knew I had all these different things I want to try. I just didn't have the mission statement clearly defined, so I sat down and wrote it out. And here is mine:

My mission in life is to live a long, happy, healthy, wealthy, and abundant life, and to travel the world empowering women everywhere!

That lit a fire in me. I knew that is what I wanted to do. When you find your "This", it is about how you feel. I felt happy with this mission statement. It also goes back to that intuition. It made me feel good to recognize that I just wanted to travel the world and empower women, and something about writing it down as a mission statement made it click and made me know that I could do it.

You can absolutely do many things under your mission statement umbrella. Under my mission statement umbrella, I am able to coach women, host empowerment retreats, run my fitness studio, volunteer and write this book. It doesn't mean that the mission statement is limited to one thing that you can do. That's not the case.

Another thing about your mission statement is that it can change. Know that! You can add on to the mission statement. Don't force it. Go with what feels good. This is your mission statement. Own it!

When you're writing this out, use words that are in your vocabulary, words that you would normally use. Don't try to use business terms unless you're a business person. Don't try to use big verbose words unless you're a research writer. Use the words that make you feel good. You can see how I write and how I talk is true to me. It's important to be 100% authentic all the time, especially when you're writing your mission statement.

You should keep your mission statement short and sweet. Now, I have seen people write out mission statements that are whole pages long, and my friend, if that's what works for you, rock it out. I like to keep mine short and sweet because that's how I roll. It makes me feel good, and it's simple. I can easily say it throughout the day, and as I always say, affirmations are huge, my friend. Sometimes the best things that you hear about yourself are the things that you say to yourself. So, if I'm feeling down and out; if I'm feeling lost; if I'm having a bad day; if I'm stressed, I will sit down, take a couple of breaths, think about it, and I say my mission statement out loud, "I am living a long, happy, healthy, wealthy, and abundant life, and I am traveling the world empowering women everywhere." This puts me back in focus and makes me feel good. It reminds me of the reason that I am doing whatever it is I'm doing at the moment.

Like I said, my good people, my mission is to really help you embrace being you. So, don't try to do what you think someone else would do. You have to really sit with it and think about what makes you feel good. Now if someone else has something that you like, you can use that, but don't base your mission on what someone else is doing or how they are doing it. Do what makes you feel good. Really take the time to think about this because this is your life, my friend. We are mapping this out because you only have one shot at life, so I really want you to take these steps.

I was just watching this movie Bucket List, and if you've never seen it, go watch it. Morgan Freeman and Jack Nicholson are both diagnosed with terminal cancer. They decide to do all the things on their bucket lists. The character played by Jack Nicholson has money out his you know what, and Morgan Freeman has the dreams and goals, just lacking the money. If you had all the money in the world and you had taken care of everybody, what would be the next thing that you would do? We'll talk about that more a little later, but just think about it. We're about to go back to the lists. You know how I am, if it's not written, it's not real, and I am all about putting pen to paper. If technology is your thing, definitely type it out after you get done, but for now, write it out. Go back into that room, that quiet space. In the movie, the character played by Morgan Freeman says that when you are faced by your higher power, you will be asked two questions.

1. Have you found joy in your life?
2. Has your life brought joy to others?

These questions will help you when thinking about your life's mission statement. Try to find what brings you joy and apply that to your mission statement. Also, think about others as much as possible because that is what our lives should be based on as well.

When you start writing this out, you'll see where you have found joy. Use that to develop your mission statement. When I was doing this, I saw that traveling, living abundantly, being healthy, and being wealthy all gave me joy, so I included those in my mission statement. I also knew that I had brought joy to those women that I was helping to empower, so I wanted to keep that as well. I do that in my speaking and in everything else that I do.

I want you to think about what gives you energy. What makes you feel empowered when you say certain things? Going back to mine, what makes me feel empowered and gives me energy is when I say that I am living a long, happy, healthy, wealthy, and abundant life, and I am traveling and empowering women. You may say that and that may not make you feel anything at all. You might not feel at all excited, but when I say that my heart seriously starts beating faster and it empowers me. It makes me realize my "Why". I know why I have to make another video, or why I have to make some other content. It makes me know why I have to go out and promote myself at a networking event or do a webinar or whatever I am doing. It just lets me know that's why I'm doing what I'm doing. I just love the way it makes me feel!

Now write down what makes you feel empowered. Brainstorm about what brings you energy and what makes you feel good. Just write it out. Keep it simple and short. Just like I said, use your own words. You want to be comfortable with it so that you can say it over and over again.

Once you have that, write down how you can use those things

that make you feel empowered to bring joy to others. Put these together to create your mission statement.

All of this comes from my heart. I want you to know that. All the stuff that I'm giving you helped me, and I want it to help you. When I'm not feeling good, when I'm sitting around asking myself stuff like, "What's the point?" I remember my mission statement, and because it's short and simple, I am able to repeat it to myself. This helps me feel better, and I want you to have the same thing, so rock it out!

Literally as I'm writing this right now, I am thinking about adding better words--words that make me feel good, words that inspire me--to my mission statement. It's always okay to improve. I'm sharing this with you, and this is the first time I've put it down with pen on paper. I am living a long, healthy, wealthy, and abundant life. I am traveling this world and excited to do it. I am closer with my man upstairs. Something to that effect at least. I am just adding words that make me feel excited, happy and fun. Somewhere in there I even want to add laughter because I think that's important. So, know that you can absolutely change it, and just make sure that it feels good. Use those juicy words!

You can also take stuff out. I remember at one point I used to always say that I want to always be busy, and I thought that was related to travel. Basically, I thought that to travel meant that I had to be in need. I wanted people to call me all the time. I wanted to be running constantly. Then there was one point when I was always back to back to back constantly running, always on the road, always traveling from work to meetings, back to work, and running errands. It was crazy, and finally I was like, "Yeah, I don't want this." I thought that I did, but once I was actually always on the go, it was different. I thought that was what being a boss babe was all about. When I was finally like, "No I don't want that at all," I took it out of my mission statement.

So, use that stuff that feels good to you, and if you write it down and then decide that you don't like something or that you want to add something, just do it. Take it out or add to it, just do what works for you.

What the mission statement does is gives you direction and guides you to finding your "This". It may not be what you do for the rest of your life, but it gives you something to work towards. Let's be real. We don't just get in a car and say, "I'm going to New York," without a plan to get there. Every step that I'm giving you is helping you find your "This.

Like I said, you can't just hop in the car and say, "I'm going to New York," with no idea how to get there. You may use Google Maps or even an old school map, but however you do it, you have a guide. Even if you get on a plane, you have to have a plan. You have to map out where it is that you're going, and just like I said, this mission statement serves as that map for helping you get to your "This".

If you don't have your life's mission statement, you are going to have whatever life throws at you. It's back to the idea of jumping in your car to go to New York without a map. You will just be on whatever road is before you. That road may take you to California or Michigan, but without a map, it is very unlikely to get you to New York. It's the same with life. You may think that you want to be an entrepreneur, but until you have taken steps to really find your path, you'll just be taking random roads that may or may not get you to where you want to go!

# Life's Mission Statement

# 9

# WHAT DO YOU WANT?

What makes YOU happy/sad on your job and personal life?

I tell people I'm a manipulator... I will manipulate you into believing in yourself that you can achieve anything you want to! The problem is the clients I work with really don't know what they truly want! That's the hard part and that's what we're going to talk about in this chapter! Trust me I get it. I know the feeling of not knowing what the fudge you really want in life and feeling like you're just going through the motions day in and day out!

Before I really sat down and did this list myself it was easy for me to say I wanted the big 5 bedroom 4 and 1/2 bath home, huge walk-in closet filled with Louis Vuitton this Chanel that, the white Audi limited edition Q7 parked in the driveway, 5 acres of land I could go on and on! Oh yes my friends I had it all mapped out to the T! But like I said when sat down and did this list I things started popping in my head like "who was going to take care of this while I'm gone?" "Am I really going to have time to enjoy this?"( because remember traveling the world and empowering women is my number one passion and purpose!) I wanted these things because that's what I was being influenced by at the time as successful and not truly what I wanted.

Now don't get me wrong I love driving nice cars and yes I do stay in very nice places when I travel to speak and vacation but I realized I don't want the commitment right now! I'm trying to travel, meet new people, eat good food, experience new cultures and I can't do that being stagnant! I'll just enjoy that lifestyle while I'm in that city or state! LOL Yes that might change in a few years when I'm ready to settle down and not travel so much but as of now I enjoy just the freedom of coming and going as I please!

 A Lot of times we base our wants and desires solely based on the fact that the next person has it. But have you really sat and thought about is that what I really want?! On top of that, have you ever really sat and thought about what you don't want? That's just as important! I'm big on energy I believe that as much as we are attracting energy to us we also have to get negative energy away from us. In order to do that you must address it and let it go that's what we're going to do here.

Like I said we must address also know what we don't want in our personal life as well as in our business and careers. Remember when I mentioned in the previous chapter I thought I wanted to always be busy, staying in meetings, running from appointment to appointment (yes I actually thought that what success looks like and that's what I wanted) but when I got that I learned real quick that was not the lifestyle for me!

You might be chasing a lifestyle or career that is bringing you negative energy. This exercise I'm going to take you through is something I learned from my mentor and I have personally done myself! I'm not going to turn this into a law of attraction book but I'm a definite believer! This was one of her attraction exercises and when I did it for myself I definitely felt better and it also gave me clarity.

When you hear of Law of Attraction you're definitely going to hear "you have to focus on the good and that's what you'll attract." Which is definitely true. Because energy gets stuck inside of your body. Just as positive energy so does negative. What this exercise is going to do is help you address that negative energy and release it so you can make room for what you truly want to attract! This exercise is also going to help you gain Clarity on your true passion and purpose!

You can do this for each area of your life. Whether it's personal, business, finances, relationships even attracting your ideal clients. As you already know I'm going to leave room at the end of this chapter so you can write in this book. But if you're reading this on the computer or for some reason you can't write in this book maybe you borrowed it from the library or it's your friends or you did this exercise last year don't let it be an excuse grab that pen and paper and let's do this!

At the top of the page I want you to write "Career" or whatever area you choose to be working on right now. Then on the front of that sheet I want you to list at least 10 things you don't want in a career(or area of choice). Your list might consist of things like I don't want to work long hours, I don't want to travel from home, I don't want to have to manage your team, I don't want to have to work overtime, I don't want to have a boss something to that effect. Don't think you're going to be attracting these things to you. Remember the purpose of this book is to help you discover your passion and purpose. In order to do that you have to get crystal clear on what it is you want. In order to do that, you also must also be clear on what you don't want!

Now we're going to turn those negatives into positives. I want you to turn the sheet over and I want you to write what you do want in your career (or whatever area you're working on) from the list you just wrote made. It's so much easier to turn what you don't want into what you truly want instead of just pulling things out of thin air. Instead of using the word "want" try using the word "desire" if that feels good to you. Throughout this whole process and everything you do it must feel good!

Now your list will go something like this I desire to work only 3 days a week while making full time pay, I desire to work close to home, I desire to work on my own, I desire to work the hours I like, I desire to be an entrepreneur! How does that feel?! It's definitely a lot easier like I mentioned before to truly see what you desire if you are clear on what you don't want. It's also a lot easier to change those negatives into positives and make room for it in your life!

Now on a blank sheet of paper (no I did not leave a space for you in this book because I want you to hang this in your room somewhere you could see it and I don't want you to rip up this beautiful book up! LOL) I want you to leave at least 4 blank lines at the top of the page for you to fill in at the end. We are going to infuse our desires with the power of love and map out what we want in that area of our life. I want you to use words that feel good (I like to say juicy words!) and put your desires together. We're going to make complete sentences that we can affirm to our self. My two favorite words are "love" and "excited" because they make me tingle on the inside! So now the above desires will read something like this...

I love only having to work 3 days a week and get full time pay!

I'm so excited I work on my own!

I love working close to home!

I'm so excited I'm in control of my schedule!

I love being an entrepreneur!

Now how does that feel?! I don't know about you but I have a smile on my face! LOL People ask me all of the time my opinions on affirmations or they say "I've been doing affirmations and they don't work!" Well keep in mind that's an affirmation is right there just by them saying they don't work! But my advice to them is they must say things that feel good to them not just because that's what someone told them to say! This process will help you out with that!

Back to the top of the page where you left the four empty lines I'd like for you to write "I'm in the process of unfolding all that I need, do, know or have to attract my ideal career" then your sentences. You'll then end the letter at the bottom of the page by writing " I love that the law of attraction is in the process of unfolding and attracting everything I need to make it happen!" BOOM! You've got clarity and a powerful affirmation attraction sheet designed just for YOU!

You'll want to read this out loud everyday twice a day right before you go to bed at night and right when you wake up in the morning! That is when our subconscious is the strongest and we can really get in there and program are mind! You are now one step closer to discovering what the fudge you are here for! Now you know what time it is go in that quiet room grab that pen and let's do this!

# What Area of My Life Am I Going to Work on First?

## 10

## THE BILLION DOLLAR QUESTION

What if YOU had all the money?

Alright, beautiful ladies, let's ask ourselves the billion dollar question. As I've mentioned throughout this book, and you'll hear me say it over and over and over again, we are not here to just pay bills. Just like I said, we definitely chase after the money. We take a job because that job is paying us just enough to get by, or we accept another job because it's paying us a little bit more than the last job was. We go into a field of work because that's what everybody else says we should do. It makes them good money, and that's what a lot of us do in life. All we do is chase that good old dollar bill.

But let's ask ourselves, "What if you had a billion dollars? What if everybody that you loved was taken care of? Your mother, your father, your siblings, your kids, your best friends, even a couple of people that you really don't like but you just know that they needed it—they are all taken care of. What if you went on all the trips that you wanted to go on, you ate all the food that you wanted to eat, you bought all the clothes that you wanted to buy, you've even pretty much stayed in every type of house that you wanted to stay in? The billion-dollar question is, "Now what?" What would you do with the rest of your life? If you didn't have to worry about your bills being paid or how you were going to pay for the next vacation, or who was going to take care of your husband if he got sick? Whatever the case may be, what are you gonna do now?

Really write that question down and you know I'm going to include a little spot in this book for you to go ahead and write that out. Would you go and volunteer and maybe help people that are in another country? Would you become a school teacher to the underprivileged kids? Would you become a mentor to those who can't afford a mentor, or a coach or to someone who maybe wants to start their own business? Would you go back to school? Would you foster kids that needed somewhere to stay? Ask yourself what would you do if you had that billion dollars because that will definitely help you with that passion and purpose in life.

Like I said, we're not chasing that paycheck. We're not chasing the money. We need to get back to finding what it is that we are here for, what is our natural talent, what makes us get up out of bed in the morning, what makes us feel fulfilled, valuable and needed? What feels like we're making a difference in the world? When you really ask yourself that billion dollar question that will absolutely help you figure things out.

For me when I really sat down and wrote this list, I wrote down many things. I wrote that I would take this trip, I would go to the spa every day, I would get my manicures and my pedicures, I would get my hair done, I would eat at all these nice restaurants and try all this food. I was writing down those things, and then when I took it back to my mentor, my coach, she really broke it down to me just like I'm breaking it down to you. She showed me that I needed to get out of the mindset of chasing material things and to really focus on my true passion and purpose. She said, Then what? After you've done the mani/pedi? After you had massages? After you've eaten all the food you wanted? After you traveled everywhere you wanted to go? What else are you going to do?"

When she asked me that, and I really went back and, as you know, I'm going to tell you once again, get in that quiet room, go out in nature, lock yourself in the bathroom if that's what you gotta do. Put some earbuds in, play some music so you can really concentrate and really think about this because your life is important and you definitely need to take it seriously.

When I did, and I sat down and I did this list I mean all kinds of things were coming up. I wrote that I would volunteer. I would help out more with kids. I would definitely like to mentor more women. I would like to go and talk to women that have been abused and didn't feel like they were valuable. I would like to give them value in their life, give them direction and let them know that they can "rock it out like a Boss," as I always say.

I would love to go and do workshops and just talk to people to empower them. I also said that I would love to read more, and I would like to improve my speaking skills. My focus then moved from being materialistic, and I really started looking inward. I'm telling you, that is what brought me to coaching. That is what brought me to doing this book right here. This is another way that I can empower women, and I love doing it. That's what brought me to speaking. That's what brought me to doing my women's empowerment retreats. When I got the focus off of the money aspect of it, I was able to think more clearly. I was able to navigate better on what it was I wanted to do with the rest of my life.

Doing these lists individually is not going to give you the answer, but once you do all of these lists and you go back over them, you will start seeing a common denominator. Your brain will start thinking a different way, and it is all about changing the mindset. That's another thing that this billion dollar question helps you with—it's changing the mindset from "We're here on this earth just to pay the bills," to "There's a bigger purpose for us." I told you I was going to say it again, and I'm sure I'll say it in again before the end of this book because I believe that is what most of us are doing.

I'm not just saying that this is the mindset here in America only. I recently got back from hosting a women's retreat in Bali, and some of the people over there have this mindset too. I loved being around them. I love their culture. I love how they still have really big family values. I love how they really give back to their higher power. I love how they did their offerings and their blessings every morning.

However, when I talked with a lot of the locals, a lot of them were saying, "Oh, I would love to come to America. I would love to come and have a big house and a nice car." I'm thinking to myself, "That is what they're starting to do. They're starting to go into this pattern of thinking that that's what makes them successful and that's what will make you happy. They have started thinking that is what will bring you joy." When I looked at their lifestyle, it really clicked. It really took me back to thinking this is how things should be.

They would have two whole families in an 800 square foot home. They don't have a lot of furniture. They don't have the washer and dryer. They don't have the big dinette table. They don't have a room for every kid. They might just have one open studio room or one extra room where the elders laid in, and most would consider that poor. We would consider them not having and them lacking, but over there they were so happy. The smiles that I saw on their faces, and the joy that I saw within them showed that they were not lacking. I thought this is how it should be versus how here we're just so focused on material things. I just wanted to throw that in there because it's not just us here in America. It's starting to become an international thing to be chasing the money.

A lot of us are chasing the big house, the big fancy car, the trips every year, the jewelry that we have, and all the material things like that thinking they bring us success. We think these things are going to make us really love our lives, but know when you discover your true passion and purpose, your "This", and you follow that, that is when you will definitely find joy. On top of that, I also want to remind you that once you find your true passion and purpose, it will bring you abundance. I am a total believer in that. My higher power— you know I'm talking about my man upstairs—definitely has blessed me, and your higher power—whatever that may be—will bless you too. After all, that's why we're here on this earth. We have to discover that, so when we do, I know that will also bring us the abundance and what we need in order to take care of ourselves.

Now I want you to take the time to think about it. Don't rush this process. Really sit there, think about if you had that billion dollars and everybody was taken care of. You've done all the things that you desire to do and you even have more than enough money to last you throughout the rest of your life. Ask yourself, "What are you gonna do? How can you give back?"

Remember the two questions in the previous chapter from the movie "Bucket List" and that's what will really help you out with this list. It's not just about us. We have got to get out of those selfish ways. We have got to get out of the way that we think that it is just all about us or it's all about the material things. We've got to quit thinking, "I'll be happy when I have this," or "I'll know I'm successful when I have that."

Now when you discover your true passion and purpose you will be able to wake up every morning and be excited to get started for your day. You won't just be going to another job, but you'll get up in the morning knowing that you're going to make a difference not only in your life but in the lives of others. When you get up every morning and your feet hit the floor, you will be ready to go out and rock your life like a Boss. It won't matter whether there's somebody paying you or not then, my friends. You will just know that you are onto something. That is what my one intention is—for this book to help you think a different way about life and to also get on the path to discovering your true passion and purpose.

Just like I said, we have to get it out of our heads. We have to put it on pen and paper, and I don't think I could have made it any easier for you besides leaving a space in this book so you can go ahead and write the list when you read these chapters. I want you to come back to this list often and know that you can also change things on this list. For instance, you might say today, "I want to foster 10 kids," but then something might happen like you might get out there and volunteer with some kids and then say, "No I don't want foster 10 kids—maybe I'll just take 2." Whatever the case may be, know that things can change. Know that your desires can change, and that's okay. You just definitely need your starting point, and this is it. Go back over it at least once to twice a year and just look at these lists that you're going through and redo them in another book if you don't have the room in here. I definitely want you to make the change, and as you already know the change starts with you.

So, I'm going to leave it right here, my good friends. We are not gonna chase that paycheck. We are not going to put ourselves in competition with each other as far as what type of car we have, what type of house we have, what type of clothes we're wearing, what type of jewelry we have on our necks and on our fingers, what type of shoes we wear on our feet, no. When all those things are already taken care of, and we're balling out with this billion-dollar question, ask yourself if you've had all of those things, "Now what?" You might actually be surprised at what pops into your head.

**I Have a Billion Dollars. Now What?**

# 11

## YES, IT'S GOING TO HAPPEN...DEATH!

What do You want people to say about YOU when you're gone?

Yes, death is going to happen to all of us, and it's time to think about what you want people to say about you when you're gone. I know this is something we don't like to talk about, and that is death, but let's face it—it's going to happen. This is just a fact, but I want to go ahead and let you know that death is nothing that you should fear. It is definitely something that you should prepare for, that way you know that you're living your life with passion and purpose. You know that your last day is going to come so prepare for it, and when it does come you want to make sure you will feel good about the life you've lived. When I say prepare, I mean you want to make sure that you live full and die empty. You want to make sure that you are preparing by doing all that it is that you want to do in this life whether you succeed or fail. This means that you took the shot and at least went out there and "beasted it out!" That's why I want to talk about death just a little bit in this chapter.

First of all, I read this book called The Tibetan Book on Living and Dying, and if you have not read that book, that is definitely a book you should read. In that book they asked the question which really woke me up one day, and the question was if you were to die tomorrow peacefully and fearlessly like you were like really straight up with yourself—like OK tomorrow is going to be my last day, are you living today in the spirit as if tomorrow were your last?

Now the first time I read that hands down without even thinking about it the answer was no. I just knew I wasn't on my right path. I knew that there was something still out there more for me. I knew that I wanted to try and experience so many things. So, without hesitation, that answer was NO! It's funny that I'm actually recording this chapter right now, I literally just looked at a journal I had (you know I'm very big on taking notes!) I actually wrote that down—the same question I just included in this book! I am currently in Bali finishing up a Women's Empowerment Retreat I lead. I was just sitting here at a coffee shop having breakfast, and the answer hands down at this time when I read the question again is yes.

Honestly, I could say that if tomorrow was my last day (even though I have so much more that I have to do) by no means am I trying to put that out here 'cause I have a lot more than I'm doing here on this beautiful earth, but I could honestly say that it was yes. I knew that I was living my passion I knew that I was out helping others I knew that I was at peace with my soul and where it was that I was going in my life. I had direction and was living with intention. I mean hands down that answer had absolutely changed. I want you to read The Tibetan Book of Living and Dying, and I want you to ask yourself that question and go ahead before you even read the book and ask the question now as you're reading my book: "if tomorrow was your last day, and you were ready to go, and you were good with that, if you know that tomorrow is going to be your last day calmly peacefully fearlessly are you living today in the spirit that you would like to be living as if tomorrow was going to be your last day?"

If your answer is no that's another reason why you have this book my friend because you need to discover that passion and purpose because death is going to happen to us, so I want you to write that down. Go ahead now and jot that down. Answer that question, and then if the answer is no, go ahead and write down ways that you want to change that to where that answer could be yes. Write down things that you can change right now or things that are coming up. For instance, write what is it that you want to change about your spirit. Write what is it you want to change about your life. I want you to go ahead in the journal part of this book and right that down now. Now the second thing I want to talk about with death is how I did this exercise and when I did it I can honestly say that it made me cry. I didn't want to do it. There were a lot of emotions that came up, but it is a good learning experience. It is a good exercise to do, and that is to write your own eulogy.

Why would you do this? I want to pose the question what do you want people to say about you when you're gone? Think about that. What do you want people to say when they're standing up giving your eulogy or when they're reflecting on you and talking about you? What is it that you want them to say? You know right now maybe your dreams you're chasing like a big car, a big house, or you know to have all this money in the bank account, or to be able to take all these lavish trips, but is that what you want people to say about you at your funeral?

Do you really want them to say, "Oh, she had a nice car; she had a nice house; she was able to take all of these trips?" There's nothing wrong with wanting those things, but my friends do you want something more than that?

This is when things really started clicking for me. When I sat down and wrote my own eulogy, I realized that I wanted people to say that I was motivating. I wanted them to say that I was inspiring. I wanted them to say that I made him laugh and that I was always there for them. I wanted them to say that I was a good friend and that I was a good daughter and a good sister and a good auntie. I mean so that's what I want you to really think about because that starts leading you to your purpose and to why you are here. You might say things like, "I want people to say that I always made them feel beautiful." Maybe you're a hair stylist or maybe you're in the makeup industry or a photographer and you're always able to make people feel beautiful with that unique gift that you have. Maybe you are a teacher and you want to be able to teach thousands of students on a certain topic or, you know, certain people to speak English. Maybe it's that you want to travel this world so you can help volunteer all over the place and give back. Maybe you want to be able to restore old history.

I don't know what your dreams are, but I really want you to sit there and think about them. It's important because those are the things that people are going to remember you by. That's your impact that you're going to make on this world. That's something that we don't think about often. It's something that we don't like to talk about, but that is what I want you to do. I'm going to leave you a section here so you can write it. I will leave it up to you how you do it.

You can do it one or two ways:

1. You can either write out your whole eulogy as if someone else where reading it.

2. You can just write a list of what you want people to say about you when you are not here.

Whatever feels easier to you that's what I want you to do on this next sheet of paper that I'm going to leave you here in this book. Like I said this is something that we don't like to talk about, but it is something that's going to happen.

Not too long ago one of my very good close cousins of mine, Pineapple, yes, that was her nickname. Don't ask, LOL. Unfortunately, she passed a few months ago at the very young age of only 43 years old. When I was at her funeral I heard the things that people said about her, and, yes, they were kind things like, "she was always there to make you laugh and she was always there to have your back 'cause she was always ready to cuss somebody out," but I knew so much more about her. I knew that there were things that she did not do but wanted to. I wish that she had had more time, and maybe if she would have thought about it like this, it would have put a fire under her butt. Maybe she would have started her passion and purpose a lot sooner.

For instance, her passion was with animals. She loved dogs, and I mean ridiculously loved dogs and animals. I'm not talking about any old dogs. I'm talking about the underdog. Pit bulls were her favorite because people look at them as aggressive dogs. They are always judged, but they are really not. They're just big babies, and when she saw strays, she would by them food or try to take them home. That was just who she was, and I always told her that she should start a nonprofit or maybe a doggy daycare or something like that. She was really passionate about animals. She would light up when she helped them.

She never put that gift to use, and now it's too late. She was also an amazing cook, and she was always talking about starting her own food truck or maybe her own restaurant or her own catering business. I believe she would have been amazing at all of them 'cause, trust me, I ate her food all the time. That was another gift and passion that was buried along with her. Her death really put a fire under my butt to just start getting it together. Like I like to say, "Get your life together!" I really needed to look in the mirror and say that to myself, and I really started living my life with more intention.

I did that eulogy exercise right before Pineapple passed away. This really opened my eyes, and I was really like, "we are not promised tomorrow." Pineapple and I used to hang out together. She was my partner in crime, as I like to say, and she was here one day and gone the next. This is just another reason why I am so passionate about helping women discover their true purpose in life because tomorrow is not promised to us, and we all deserve to live a good life.

We all deserve to live within our passion and our purpose. We all deserve to live with intent. You want to bless somebody else with the purpose and passion that you have—that you're naturally born with—now is the time to start because you might be holding that blessing back from somebody else who needs that gift. This is also why I decided to write this book and do what I do. I believe if I can continue to help women discover their true passion and purpose and why they're here and turn their lives around and have them believe in themselves, I am doing my job.

I know I was put here to empower, here to motivate, here to have you believing in yourself so you can discover your true passion and purpose. That is my mission. That is how I want to give back to others, and that is what I want people to say about me. I want you to also think about that because it's not all about us we are also here on this earth to impact others to give to somebody else. Think about that long and hard. How do you want to affect the lives of others? When you think about that include that in your eulogy or include that in your list and maybe that'll help you write this out a little bit easier.

As always, make sure that you're somewhere quiet—somewhere where you can really think about this—because your life is something serious. This whole book is something serious. It is to discover your true passion and purpose. 'Cause, like I've said repeatedly, we only have one shot at this beautiful thing called life.

Now after you've written out your eulogy or after you've written out your list, I want you to think about what are the steps that you can now do to make this happen. So, think about the different ways that you can make this happen. Ask yourself what applies to you: "How can I empower people? I can write books. I can do webinars. I can do classes. I can do workshops. How can I help out animals? I can volunteer. I can open up a shelter. I can work at a vet's office. How can I help out those that are hungry? I can start a nonprofit. I can go volunteer at a nonprofit. I can look up a video about nonprofits."

We can all start somewhere. Half the battle is getting your mindset right, but the next step is to take the next step. Once I get you to start looking at your life differently, it's time to start taking those little steps to really discovering and living your true passion and purpose.

Remember my friends, you have got this, and I'm going to leave you with this. Like I've said before, one of my favorite quotes is Mark Twain's quote,

"The two best days of your life are the day that you were born and the day you discover why."

Are you ready to make that discovery?

**What Do I Want People to Say about Me When I'm Not Here?**

# 12

## IT'S NEVER TOO LATE!

No matter the age, what you've been through, etc., there is still time.

Okay, ladies, so this book is geared towards my beautiful women 30 and over because that is when I feel like you're ready to either make a change, take a chance, or really take life seriously. If you're anything like me, in my late teens, heck, in all of my 20s, you couldn't tell me anything. I knew what I was supposed to do in life and where it was that I was supposed to go. You couldn't tell me anything I had it all figured out!(at least I thought I did) The last thing I was thinking about is finding what they call your life's purpose.

Right around your late 20's early 30's is when I believe a lot of us truly start listening to that pull that's inside of us. This is when we really look around and say, "Oh, it's time to get real and take my life seriously," if it's not going in the direction you believe it should be going in. And, just like I said, yes, this book is for ladies over 30, but it doesn't matter 30, 40, 50, 60--even in your 70s and later than that--you can definitely still find your "This." If at any age you are still feeling that there is a pull or a call inside of you and you're not going in the direction you should be, the reason you're having that feeling is that you need to do something about it.

For instance, there's a lot of people that I've been researching that didn't discover their passion until after 30 years old. At 39, Julia Childs wrote her first cookbook and didn't start her first cooking show until she was 51. Vera Wang--I'm sure you know of her-- at 23, she gave up her dream of being a competitive figure skater and became editor of Vogue for 15 years, but when she didn't get the job as editor-in-chief, she quit. She didn't design her first dress until the age of 40, but look at her now. Samuel L Jackson didn't get his first movie role until 42. Morgan Freeman didn't get his first major role until 52. Grandma Moses didn't start her painting career until she was 76.

My favorite example is my man, Mr. Colonel Sanders. Oh, I'm sure you've heard of KFC! At 20, his wife left him and took his daughter. He joined the military. When he got out he was in law school, and he got rejected from becoming a lawyer. He then tried to be an insurance salesman, which he failed at. After than, he went on to become a cook and dishwasher. He retired at 65 and was getting a check for $105 a month from the government. This really put him in a bad place. He was even suicidal.

He went to write a suicide letter under a tree one day, and as he was sitting under the tree writing the suicide letter, something inside of him was still pulling at him. Instead of completing that letter, he started writing what he would've done with his life if he was able to start over. When he did that, when he started making that list (Sound familiar, my friends?), new ideas started popping in his head. Then his love for cooking came out of the list. He just started writing, and he got his fried chicken idea. He borrowed $87 to get a fryer and the ingredients to make his recipe.

It still wasn't easy from there, my friends. He had to go out and promote his recipe to friends and family, people he knew, and restaurant owners. He got rejected 1009 times. Yes, my friends, 1009. To be honest, I don't see how my man did it because I'm not even sure if I'm that strong at this point of me writing this book to get rejected 1009 times and still pursue that passion, but at that 1010th time, he asked, and he got a yes. With that KFC was born. He became a full-time billionaire at the age of 88.

See my friends, it is never too late to go after your dreams. Just try and start the process and do what I guess what these kids nowadays call a life hack. You'll get there sooner than the age of 65.

I remember a time I was doing a workshop at a yoga studio. It was my vision board workshop, which has some of the steps that I give you here to help discover your life's purpose. I was asking the crowd "what did they enjoy doing in their free time?" "what brought them joy?" There was a lady who pulled me to this side and asked if she could talk to me. She started explaining how she felt. She said she "wanted to get up and leave the workshop because she felt like she was too old to make change."

I asked her what brought her joy and where could she see herself in the future. This made her almost cry. She explained to me that all of her life she's always been the caregiver of her family and her friends. She and her husband were married for over 50 years, and he had passed three years prior. She was at the age of 66, and she said it had been so long since someone had asked her what she enjoyed doing and what brought her joy. She said it had been even longer then that she had been asked about where she see could herself in her future.

She kept explaining to me and telling me how she just really enjoyed taking care of the family and really enjoy taking care of her friends. I started her on the process of the things that I told you in this book, and she started explaining to me how she really liked working with kids. She also had the opportunity to work with family members and friends and family that had kids with disabilities, so I gave her the idea of just going to volunteer at a local hospital or working with an organization that specializes in helping special needs children.

She sent me an email a couple months later and told me that she started working with a local organization here in Florida with at-home care department with kids with special needs, and it has brought her joy like no other. She even told me she's getting paid for it, and she hadn't gotten paid for anything in over 50 years! She says that she has definitely found her passion and found her spark for life again.

See my friends, it's never too late. I also have another client who just turned 73. She has a very similar story. Her husband had passed, but she actually got back into dating again. She got her a new boo, and she had been doing a lot of traveling. She still felt like something was missing. After going through the process with her, she sparked up again. Her passion is teaching, so she has gone back to teaching online to kids overseas. She says she absolutely loves it and never thought that in her 70s she would be teaching again or using technology to do it! She said she was not computer savvy, so, once again see my friends, it's never too late.

I typically work with ladies between the ages of 30 - 50 years old. I notice that the ladies are coming to me because they are ready to step into their greatness, and they still have that feeling of they should be doing something more. That feeling, that pull inside will always be there until you address it. Like I said, my friends, the sooner you do these steps, you will be living your passion your purpose, and you will know that you have found your "This."

Maybe you had a health scare or you just went through a divorce or a bad breakup and you're having to start over again, or maybe you just tired of seeing your friends and family members really step into their passion and their greatness, and you're ready to do the same. You're ready to make the decision to listen to your intuition to follow the steps. You'll be living the life you were meant to be before you know it.

I can speak from personal experience like I've mentioned before right around 30 is when it happened to me. I was going through that breakup. I moved away from Florida when I was 18, and I thought I would never move back. After I went through that break up, I had to make that phone call to come back home. When I came back to Florida, I started doing what I've always done pretty much in my life—bartending and waiting tables because that's what I knew.

I started having this pull inside of me just like I said at the beginning of the book. I had hit my highest weight, and I knew something inside, which is confidence, wasn't there. My self-esteem was definitely low, and I knew that I was destined for something besides doing what I was just doing. There were times when I felt like it might be too late, but when I decided to get a coach and find joy and do the steps is when I started to change. Even when I opened up my own studio I thought that

that was it for a while—this is what I'm supposed to do. I thought I was just supposed to be there at the studio empowering these ladies and helping them lose weight just like I had done, but still there was that pull. There was still something inside of me telling me that I was supposed to do something different.

When I really started exploring that's when the coaching was brought to me. It was not only me getting coached myself, but me becoming a coach, and with that speaking opportunities came to me. I started doing a lot of traveling, which is something I have always had a passion for.

When I started making it happen, that's when I stepped into my true purpose. Now I am feeling my best –traveling the world to empower women everywhere. Yes, I have my hands in many different things—being an instructor at the studio, an owner, hosting webinars, retreats and workshops, doing different speaking engagements, and being part of different organizations. But all of them align with my true passion and purpose, which is to empower women everywhere. That is my goal for you, my friends, to really live this life you want to live, so when you die you go out of here with no regrets.

Two beautiful women in my life helped me to see this as well. One was my great-grandmother who passed at the age of 98. That was the first funeral that I had been to that I didn't cry one tear because she always told me how happy she was. She always had a smile on her face. She just looked happy all the time. The other one is my beautiful grandma who is still with us. This year, Lord willing, she will be 95 years old. She always has a smile on her face as well and she's always been a hard worker. These two women in their old age were and are still active and they would tell stories about their life that they lived with joy.

They really enjoyed the life that they had. They went after their dreams even when they got older. Both of these beautiful ladies remind me it's never too late and to smile!

It's never too late to step into your right path. We owe it to ourselves to discover what our passion and purpose and what this life is all about. I am reminded of a quote I just posted the other day. Charlie Brown and Snoopy were sitting by the water, and Charlie Brown says to Snoopy, "Snoopy you only live once." Snoopy replies, "We only die once. You live every day."

That is critical for this book, my friends. Remember that while you are still here you should be living your true passion and purpose. It is only too late when you're gone.

## 13

## F**K WHAT THEY SAY!

People will talk about YOU and knock your dreams, but F**K what they say!

So, we're at the end of this book, and by now you should definitely have a lot of ideas on the direction of where you want to take your life and how to start your next chapter! At this point, if I have not said this already, I want you to watch who you tell your dreams or goals to.

Why? Because people around you will start talking. They've seen how you've lived your life, and if you're making a change, whether it's for the good or bad, they are gonna say something about the situation. I hate to tell you my friends, nine times outta ten, if you are setting goals that are outside of your comfort zone and outside of theirs as well. Some of your friends and closest family members are gonna doubt you. They are going to say things like, "Oh, she can't do that. Who does she think she is?" Or, "You know I've seen her fail so many times in these other things how is she gonna make this happen?"

How do I know this? Because it has happened in my life when I was going after my dreams and goals. I tell people all the time just F what they say. Let me break it down to you. People are gonna talk about you when you're doing good, and people are gonna talk about you when you are doing bad. So, you might as well go and do the thing, my friends. Nine times out of ten, they don't really mean any harm. Like I said, they just don't see your vision.

They don't see you any different because you've always been doing the same things around them. In their minds, you know, they are still living the life that ya'll have always lived. Just be okay with that. Just watch who you're telling your dreams or goals to. Because there's gonna be so many other negative things that will happen along the journey to really stepping into your greatness. You don't need the negative energy or influences of your friends and family members. You don't need people around you telling you how much you can't do it and they don't believe that you should be able to do it.

I remember when I started my business I had people that were close to me telling me "You shouldn't do this. You should just go back to bartending and doing what you've always done. At least you were making money." You know it really did hurt me, and it really brought me down.

I really realized when I stopped looking for the approval of others, and I just started saying, "F**K it. F**K what you say. I'm just gonna rock it out like a boss," that is when I really started moving forward. I really started fulfilling my dreams, and that is what I want for you.

To be honest, some of the people that are around you, they're really hating on you because they're jealous of you because they didn't take that step. They're really jealous that you were brave enough to take the step to step outside your comfort zone, to go back to school, to start that business, to start losing weight, to start saving money, to buy your house, to buy a new car, or whatever the case may be.

I'm just gonna say it my good friends, it's because they're jealous that you did take the steps, and they didn't have the courage to do so for themselves. It is what it is. I'm not saying that ALL of them are like that, but there are those types of people out there! And that's the reason that they're hating on you. And yes, I get it, we're humans. We do care what other people think to an extent, but we have to stop that!

I really believe it started when we were little because we always asked for permission and looked for validation in some type of way. When we were kids, we had to ask our parents if we could do this you, go there, do that. We were also trying to get approval from them. We tried to prove ourselves to them by making good grades or getting the good job or being the good kid or whatever the case may be. Then we started going to school and we were always asking for permission or validation from our teachers and our peers and things like that. Once we got into the working field, we had to ask for permission, and we went looking for validation from our boss and our coworkers.

When you start going outside of your comfort zone or you start going for your dreams, your goals, your passion, your purpose, you know it is just a subconscious thing that's kind of like already seeped into our heads because we're looking for that validation. We're looking for that permission. Like, "Is this okay?" We worry about what other people say about us, and, you know, if they talk about us. It makes us think, "Maybe I need to back away and not do that." The fear sets in, and then we don't go after our dreams, our passion and purpose.

I'm telling you, you have to F**k what they say and just do it anyway. Stop looking for that permission. Stop looking for that validation, you know. You are living this life for you. It's up to you to give back, to use your natural talent, to find your true passion, to seek your purpose, and to make a difference in this world.

You know, it's up to you to leave a footprint for whenever you're not here anymore like we talked about in the chapter on death. Definitely stop it looking for approval my friends. It's something that has subconsciously been put in your head, start using those affirmations like I told you. Start by saying, "I am enough. I am worth this. I am discovering my true passion. I am finding my purpose. I am going after my passion and my purpose." That's what this book is all about -- you discovering your true passion and purpose, letting go of the fear, not giving a F**k what other people say, and actually doing it!

You can start with today. Just pick one thing that maybe you wanted to do but you worried about what your parents were gonna say, what your coworkers were gonna say, what your family was gonna say, what your spouse was gonna say. Just pick one thing whether it's a simple thing, like I was going to upload a Facebook post that was inspirational or do a blog or do a video or something like that, but I was always worried about what everybody was gonna say. Today is the day, my friends. I want you to go ahead and do that.

Maybe you were gonna tell your spouse that you wanted to start doing yoga or take a ballroom dance class or a pole fitness class. (Oh yeah, did you know I owned a Vertical Pole Studio?

Surprise!) Whatever you might've wanted to do but you were afraid to tell your spouse because you were worried about what he was gonna say or do. Do that!

What these small wins are gonna do is you're gonna start getting to the point where you see you can do all these little things, and you're gonna be ready to go into those bigger things. You're going to overcome that fear, do those little things, and you're gonna say, "Okay, well, I'm still here," and you're gonna be ready to go into those bigger things those bigger goals that purpose that passion and what it is that you're here to do. So, just pick one thing today, my friends, as you are reading this and go ahead and make today the day that you're gonna start changing your life around.

Everything that you do, as I mentioned so many times, starts with your mind. Everything starts with you taking action. Start with doing something very small that you can go ahead and do. Ask that boss for that day off, I mean, maybe that's even something that's kind of held you back because you were afraid of what other people were gonna say. Ask for that raise, for that promotion that you deserve, but you were scared of what everybody else was gonna say. Whatever you knew that was your passion, whatever you needed that was your purpose, but you let that fear hold you back, go ahead and do that.

We have to stop worrying about what people say, I'm gonna say this over and over again, because that holds us back from stepping into our greatness, from stepping into our true passion and purpose. We don't do the video, we don't ask for the raise, we don't start the diet, we don't go back to school, we don't start the business, whatever the case may be, because we're worried about what other people will say.

We have got to stop that and just, like I say, let those small victories, those small wins get you to a point of confidence, not cockiness, but just to a point of knowing that you can do it. And even if you fail, just keep trying. That's when you really start getting to the point where you don't care what other people say.

It doesn't matter if you have failed, but that you're still here, you're still trying. That's when confidence will get built up. That's when you will become empowered, and I'm telling you you will find your true passion and purpose and step into that. It only takes that one time, that one success, that one victory to get you where you really truly discover that you are on your right path, my friends. I am telling you I know what it feels like. I know how it feels to let fear hold us back from doing "the thing" from stepping into our greatness.

A quote that I think of is "If you always care about what other people think you will always be their prisoner." Lao Tzu said that. That is so true. If you always worry about what everybody else is thinking about you, my dear friends, they have control over you.

You have to remember that we are the co-creators of our life. We are the ones that have to make it happen. It is our job to discover our true passion and purpose, why it is we're here and to step into our greatness, and if we don't hold onto that, we are becoming somebody else's prisoner because we worried about what they say about us. I mean, what the "fudge", we are not in school anymore.

It's so funny, well, no it's not funny because I've been there. I get it, but I see so many women and even men that really worry about what other people think about them. I will say that there is a study that shows that men don't care as much as women do.

You know, it is true. Women can be emotional, and we do kind of wear our heart on our sleeve. We do worry about what other people say about us, and men (not all of them just like not all women) they just don't care and they'll do it anyways, and when they fail, it's just like whatever. They'll keep going.

Because women are 95% of my audience, if not more, I just really want us to be able to not worry about what the next person says about us so we can really let go of all of the negative thoughts and worrying about what they say. Just like I said, we let that fear hold us back from taking that next step, and we sit in our comfort zone. Then we start doing the same thing over and over and over again, and we truly don't step into that greatness and find that passion, find that purpose in life.

You're in control of your reaction. You're not in control of other people, what they think, what they say, what they do. That is life. Who you are in control of is YOU. You are in control of taking that step outside of your comfort zone, not caring what they say, and continuing on with your goals and dreams. Always remember that. Let those people talk. Like I mentioned before, they're gonna talk about you whether you're doing good or whether you're doing bad. Let that be. Recognize that. Know that. Understand that. And be okay with that.

What would you do if heard them talking about you? What would you do about that situation? Would you let it hold you back? Would you be okay? Go ahead and act as if they are already talking about you, so you can prepare yourself for that. Write it down. Ask yourself, what is the worst thing they can say about whatever situation? What is your response? How does it make you feel? If you are already prepared for the worst, then you will know how you are gonna handle the situation. Go ahead and be proactive about the situation, my good friends, but just don't let it hold you back.

People will only mess with your head if you let them. It is that mindset. Don't let them have control over you. Don't become that prisoner that I was talking about in that quote. Really take control of yourself and believe that you deserve this. Know that you are destined for greatness. Believe that you can become that person that you see in the future. You can become that person that you are aspiring to be.

Don't look at what you did in the past and things like that because that's just, like I said, why some of the people around you talk about you. You have to change your mindset. You have control of your reactions. You have control of your life. You are the co-creator of this. Go ahead and make that change into who you truly are. Live your purpose. Live your passion.

Maybe I'm being a little biased by making this next statement, but I really do feel entrepreneurs have the worst time of worrying about what everybody else will say. For one, I am an entrepreneur, and not only that just being an entrepreneur in general we have to step outside of the normal box. We're not going to that normal 9 to 5. We don't just go to school, get that degree, go to to the job, get that paycheck every two weeks or whatever the case may be.

In the beginning we're already stepping outside of our comfort zone, especially when we grew up in a "normal" family that believes in the 9-5 way of life. I know because that is how my family is. My family is very much in the mindset of you go to school, get your education, get a job and that's what it is.

My immediate family especially didn't understand actually going out there and not having any money while busting your butt working 60+ hours a week to build the business and not making any money. They didn't understand going in debt, bills getting behind and the time it takes to build a business. As far as entrepreneurship, I get that.

And then when you do get that business and you're starting that, there are just the ideas that you have to come up with and branch out and do different things because you have to keep up with your competitors, you really just have to put yourself outside of your comfort zone. Speaking as an entrepreneur, I do get the fact that you're really going to have to really work hard to not worry about what other people say.

You might have to go to a networking event. You might have to ask for a big meeting. You may want to meet that certain director because you're trying to get into the film industry. Whatever the case, if you worry what other people are talking, like, "Who does she think she is? We've never heard of her, but here she is asking for this meeting over here," and you really let that get in your head, you're going to let that hold you back.

Maybe you're wanting to become a hairstylist or a makeup artist and you want to talk to the top makeup artist or whatever the case may be like the top business hair salon owner in your area, people might start saying, "Who does she think she is being able to talk to them?" When you're wanting to start a business like me, that may happen. For instance, I was bartending and waiting tables, and people said, "Oh, now you want to open up a fitness studio, and you want to become a coach, like what is that about?"

I'm a little biased by saying this, but I really want to stress this to my entrepreneur boss babes out there: you are gonna have a lot of talk, you are gonna have things because just in general we're getting that slack because being an entrepreneur is taking us outside of our comfort zone. We always have to stretch ourselves anyways to stay in the top of our game, so there's gonna be that talk. You're gonna have to learn, my friends, to get over it and not worry about it.

Just the thought of worrying about what other people say about you, entrepreneur or not, whatever the case may be, it still goes back to the fear. I also want to touch on this for a moment. There's this one quote that I really love, and I talk about it all the time. It says something to the effects that the graveyard is the richest place on earth. Why? It's because it's here that you will find all the hopes and dreams that were never revealed, the books that were never written, the songs that were never sung, the inventions that were never shared, the cures that were never discovered, all because someone was too afraid to take the first step with the problem or determine to carry out their dream. That was by my man Les Brown, who is an amazing motivator and mentor, love him, of mine.

But that is so true, and that goes back to the fear and that we worry about what people say about us. If we didn't care what someone would say about us, we would do just about anything. We would be like that child that just keeps doing what she wants because kids don't care what anyone says about them. They're fearless and will try just about anything.

As adults, we allow that fear to hold us back, and it kinda goes back to the chapter that I was talking about feeling the fear and do it anyway, but this fear usually comes from what people are saying about us. Don't leave this earth with your true passion your true purpose going to the graveyard with you. You need to bless us with the gifts that you were blessed with and not worry about what these fools say about us out here.

Now I just want to leave you ladies with this: If I would have let the opinion of others hold me back, I would not be where I'm at today, and that is writing this amazing book (I think it is) and actually fulfilling my dreams of traveling the world and actually empowering women whether it's through my speeches, teaching my classes, doing workshops or webinars, I really do feel like I have discovered where it is that I need to be, and I want you to do the same. We can't live our lives on the opinion of others.

Remember these three steps to do to help you move towards your passion and purpose. My goal for this book is to definitely help you start brainstorming and figuring that out. I want you to

1. Write down what is the worst that could happen for going after your passion or purpose that way you go ahead and be prepared for whatever negative feedback and talk and whatever other people may say about you so you can just not give AF.

2. Then I want you to pick that one thing today, my friends, that you've been scared of the opinion of others holding you back and do it. It can be something small just like I said. It can be as small as a Facebook post or a blog or a video. It can be asking for that day off from your boss or telling your spouse you want to do something that they might think that you're a fool for doing. Go ahead and do that one thing today because that will build your confidence and help you get closer to your passion and your purpose.

3. Stop caring about what other people will say. Don't forget you have to change that mindset!

Like I said everything that we do in life absolutely starts in our mind. So, we are gonna have to choose not to worry about what other people say about us. Know that we are the co-creators of our life. We are the bosses and the captains of our ships. All we can do is control our reactions. We can't control what other people say about us because they gonna talk as you know.

They talked about all kinds of people that are doing big things right now. They talked about Oprah Winfrey and Cardi-B, (that's so funny I just said Oprah and Cardi-B together) but they are very successful. They talked about people that are actually changing lives every day on a daily basis and these people are still here. They are thriving and they are doing the thing in them and their passion and purpose, my good friends. I mean even the stars that are out here, like Madonna, Denzel Washington, Will Smith, Jada Picket Smith, they talked about these people, but these people have got to the point where they don't care. They don't live their lives based on what other people say. That is what I want you to do, my friends. F**k what they say, do it anyway. Step into your passion and purpose, go out there and rock your life like a Boss!

**What Am I Worried that People Will Say If I Do My Thing?**

# 14

## YOU GOT THIS!

Closing Inspiration and Motivation

Here we are beautiful ladies at the end of the book. If you thought you were going to get here and you were going to hear the bells ringing and have that big aha moment but it didn't happen. I have news for you, my friends it's not that easy!

The purpose of this book is to definitely get you to think about things that you haven't in a long time. This book is to help you to start brainstorming and coming up with new ideas to see things more clearly in the direction of where you want to go in your life. But in all in all honesty you have to get out there and put things in action! You have to listen to your intuition, be still and listen to what is coming to you and follow the path that is already laid out there for you!

Like I said I'm a firm believer that we all are born with a true purpose on this Earth. There is a reason why we are here and as I mentioned over and over again it's not just to pay the bills! You owe it to yourself to discover what that is! You don't want to go through life with thoughts of what if I would have tried this?" Or "what if I would have went back to school?" Or "what if I would have started that business?" Or "what if I would have moved overseas?" You know your "what if's" We only have one shot at the beautiful thing called life my friends. And if any of those thoughts or anything along that line pops into your head it was given to you for a reason!

Everyone does not have the same dreams as you, the same thoughts as you or the same desires that you have. And that is for a reason. That is your passion and purpose that is your reason for being here and you need to go out there and go after it!

Don't live your life just going through the motions or doing things because that's how you see everybody else around you doing them. Don't become that check the box girl! I was watching an interview with Oprah and Michelle Obama. Michelle was telling Oprah how she became the check the box girl. Meaning her family wanted her to go to a good college check, get a good job (she became an attorney) check, marry a good man (I mean how much better can you get she did marry the president of the United States!) check, have a family (as we know she had two beautiful daughters) check. But on the inside she said she knew she was not going in the direction she was meant to.

 Most of us on the outside would look at her and consider her successful. She was one of the top attorneys at a prestigious law firm in Chicago, had a good husband, had a great family but still she had that pull inside that let her know there was something more out there for her. She mentioned when she walked out of that attorney's office on her last day it felt like one of the best days of her life! she was able to begin her true passion of philanthropy work with young girls. She knew in her heart and her soul that she was on the right path.

As I've mentioned throughout this book you will have this feeling like no other when you are on your right pass. I kept having this pull inside of me for years until now. Now that I'm going after my true passion and purpose I no longer feel it. Now I feel excitement and joy every day that I wake up that I'm able to empower and motivate women to step into their greatness and discover their true passion and purpose.

That's not to say that things would not change in the future, remember it's okay for things to change. But as of right now I know that I am on the right path! And that is what I desire for you! I want you to wake up every morning with a smile on your face and ready to beast out the day because you love what it is that you are doing! It brings you joy, you feel like your talents and skills are being used, your doing what you love and it feels so damn good while your doing it!

Okay my friends you must take this process of discovering your true passion and purpose seriously! I mean it is our lives we're talking about anyways! Trust the process! Be open to new ideas, new ways of thinking, new ways of living and new role models. Your thought process will change as you're going through this as well.

Just a quick example of how your thought process will change. I remember when I used to watch Oprah and honestly I wasn't a big fan. I used to think that she was a butt kisser, thought she was better than everybody else and just doing things to impress white people! Yes that is just how small-minded and ignorant my thought process was before I change! Now I'm one of her number one fans!

I love and respect her story of how she was raised and overcame many obstacles in her life! She was a fighter who knew her true passion and purpose! She didn't let anyone get in her way white, black, chinese, or any other nationality for that matter! She knew that her passion and purpose was to teach and that is what she has been doing all these years. Yes she has done it on many platforms. With her TV show, interviews, radio, podcast, magazine, TV station and I could go on! And she has inspired and taught many people myself included!

Okay my friend's I'm going to wrap this up. Because the quicker you get finish reading this book the quicker you can go ahead and start doing these steps and discovering what the "fudge" it is you are here for!

As cliche as this might sound I can't help but say it "if I can do it you can do it too!" If I can go from being the girl that used to party all night, sell drugs, get in trouble with the law and not give a "fudge" what anybody else said about her. To being a woman who is a business owner, motivational speaker, retreat leader and author (just to name a few of my titles) then I know you can absolutely do it as well! Will it be easy? Not all the time my friend. Will it be worth it? Absolutely!

Since you bought this book I'm going to take it as a sign that you're ready to discover what the "fudge" you are here for. You bought this book for a reason now put it into action! You already know we're not getting any younger. Tomorrow is not promised to any of us! As I've quoted "you want to live full and die empty" And once you discover your true passion and purpose you will be able to live the life you were meant to!

I'm going to go ahead and tell you now there will be times that you will doubt yourself. You are going to run into some challenges and obstacles along the way. But that is just what they are challenges and obstacles! You can definitely overcome them I have no doubt! And when you do you'll be stronger because of it!

Keep your why in front of you, see the vision of your life how you desire it, set your goals and go after them daily! And as I always tell you ladies "if you're at a point in your life where you're not quite believing in yourself, no worries I believe in you! And sometimes you just have to believe in the belief that others have in you before your own belief kicks in!"

Now go out there and rock your life like a BOSS!

# ABOUT THE AUTHOR

Mia is the Owner of Beautiful You Studio in Pensacola FL. She's also a ICF Certified Empowerment Coach and Motivational Speaker. After overcoming her past struggles, she found her passion for empowering women to do the same! So they can step into their greatness and go after their dreams! Mia specializes in helping women discovering their true Passion & Purpose. She loves being on stage and motivating women to believe in themselves! She has spoken at Women's Empowerment Expo's & Conferences, Black Heritage Festival, The Success Summit in California and the American Breast Cancer Survivors Dinner just to name a few. As well as hosting Women's Empowerment Retreat's throughout the US and just coming back from her first International Retreat in Bali! She loves to volunteer in her community and networking as much as possible.

She loves to volunteer in her community and networking as much as possible, she is also the Leader of the local Lean In Group in Pensacola (Lean In/Own It). In her free time, she loves to travel, eat, laugh, hang outdoors, watch sports and brunch with her girls!

"If you would've told me this would be my life 5 years ago I would've told you that sounds nice but you're crazy fool! But here I am really meaning it when I say IF I CAN DO IT YOU

CAN DO IT! (Laughing) I strive to show women everyday how they can do the same! So they can step into THEIR greatness and rock their life like a BOSS!" ~ Mia

beyouwithmia.lifecoach@gmail.com

www.facebook.com/groups/beyouwithmiacoaching

Join me for my free Mindset Reset 5 Day Transformation!

Over a course of 5 days, I'll be teaching you how to reset your mindset. You will practice SIMPLE ways to worry less, quiet anxiety, get rid of your limiting beliefs so you can beast out and be ready to crush your goals. But before you start setting those goals you need to first declutter and reset your mind. If you don't know how to do that, don't worry I Got You! Sign Up Below and I'll see you on the inside!

Once you learn the skill of resetting your mind will be yours forever. Let's Do This!

http://bit.ly/5DayMindsetReset

Made in the USA
Coppell, TX
26 August 2024

36498249R00066